Playing with Time

WOMEN WRITING FOR PERFORMANCE

compiled and edited by Colleen Chesterman, with Virginia Baxter
Playworks

© Playworks 1995

Playworks,
PO Box 1523,
Darlinghurst, NSW 2010.

Phone (02) 262 3174
Fax (02) 262 6275

ISBN 0-646-26020-0

Designed by Dana Kocanov and James Norton
Printed in Australia by Fast Books, a division of Wild &Woolley Limited, Glebe, NSW

about this survey

Playworks, a national organisation committed to nurturing new women writers, encouraging new forms of writing for performance and supporting and developing the work of more experienced women writers, was established in 1985.

To celebrate our tenth anniversary and to acknowledge the contributions of women as writers to Australia's performing arts, Playworks thought it timely to assess how women writers had experienced the past ten years. We were particularly interested to find out whether there had been any marked improvement in the opportunities for women to have their work professionally performed during the ten years of our operation.

We wanted to hear the individual experiences of women writing for theatre and performance, any factors related to gender affecting their work and its success in reaching production and any special advantages and obstacles they may have experienced as women writing for performance. Playworks wanted to document stories of success and any problems or challenges.

Since one of our questions related to success in gaining development support, we decided to assess the grants made to women writers over the past ten years by the Australia Council, compared with the number of grants made to male writers and whether these were concentrated in any particular areas. We asked the Australian National Playwrights' Centre and Currency Press to provide their perspectives.

The final strand of the survey was to document the works for performance and plays written by Australian women performed by professional theatre companies, which received funding from Commonwealth and State arts funding bodies. We asked them to show the works performed year by year over the past ten years, comparing the number written by women to the number written by men. We also asked companies to document the creative and decision-making positions held in their company by women, to consider their experience in producing plays or works for performance by women and point to any areas where Playworks could assist.

Although there have been a number of useful statistical analyses of the situation of women working in the arts, this survey provided a new opportunity to consider the lived experiences of women working in one particular field. This document enables us to celebrate what Australian women writers for theatre and performance have achieved and reflect on the ways they can be encouraged to develop further.

Acknowledgments

This publication and the research survey which produced it would not have been possible without a grant from the Women's Grants Program of the NSW Department for Women which allowed Playworks to begin research in NSW and an additional grant from the Australia Council, Strategy and Communications Branch, to extend that research Australia-wide.

Initial thanks must go to all the women writers and practitioners who participated in the survey, some of them with extremely detailed and thoughtful analyses of their experiences. Sincere thanks as well to all the performing arts companies who combed their archives and completed surveys.

This publication rests on the dedicated work of researchers who analysed and followed up the questionnaires. Alison Lyssa undertook the mammoth task of interpreting much of the data from writers and produced a sensitive and considered report. In each state and territory, women writers followed up data, interviewed companies and burrowed in libraries to prepare detailed assessments of the past ten years. Considerable thanks for their thorough work and the time they devoted to the task to Belinda Bradley in Tasmania; Sarah Brill in Western Australia; Josephine Fleming in Queensland; Tanya Gerstle in NSW; Verity Laughton in South Australia; Fiona Navilly in the Australian Capital Territory; Suzanne Spunner in the Northern Territory and Jennie Swain in Victoria. Helen Swan devoted her skills to analysing the tables and statistics; Catherine Wyburn prepared biographies. Considerable assistance on the final draft was provided by Virginia Baxter.

Layout and design was undertaken by Dana Kocanov and James Norton with the generous cooperation of Leong Chan, Design Department, University of NSW College of Fine Arts. Playworks thanks them for the contribution they provided to making the final publication so attractive.

Assistance on the project, through either testing the questionnaire, contacting writers or reading the final draft, was provided by Playworks directors and administrators Clare Grant, Caitlin Newton Broad and Sally Richardson and by Andrea Aloise, Kathie Ashton, Eliza Chidiac, Jennifer Compton, Eva Cox, Cris Edmonds-Wathen, Keith Gallasch, Noelle Janaczewska, Deborah Leiser, Peta Tait, Margaret Williams and Angharad Wynn-Jones.

Statistics were provided by Jeanette Sharp and Abdullah Eyssa of the Australia Council. Advice on research on women writers for performance was given by Ron Layne of the Strategy and Communications Branch of the Australia Council.

For its ongoing work on behalf of women writing for performance, Playworks acknowledges the support of the Australia Council, through its Performing Arts and Literature Boards, and the NSW Ministry for the Arts.

Colleen Chesterman

celebrating playworks

Ros Horin, founding artistic director, Playworks:

The idea for Playworks came to me after the (1982) Women and Arts Festival, as many women writers had a negative experience from the one-off showing of their work. I felt something more was needed, more long-term, where women writers could develop in a protected low-profile environment before emerging into the public arena. We had to see more images of women on stage and to assist women writers by finding a process that was flexible, enduring, with a depth of development. So I called together a group of friends, artists, and together we workshopped what it might be...

Virginia Baxter, current Playworks chair:

Playworks had many mothers, all theatre practitioners. It was born of a desire to see the work of women writers up there vying for attention with the work of male writers for performance. Its birth was relatively easy by all accounts, well and truly planned and its growth over the first ten years has been rigorously monitored. Experimental approaches to rearing have been favoured over 'tried and true' formulas. At ten, Playworks may look a little different but her mothers recognise in the organisation the fruit of their labours.

In 1995 Playworks is still run by practitioners and maintains the same careful and flexible approach to writer development. The Playworks process is inclusive, encouraging an interplay of ideas between the broadest possible range of writers and theatre workers. Playworks promotes writers themselves as much as their plays and texts. It provides an emotional and intellectual forum for the exchange of ideas. The only slightly worrying element is that though Playworks has now entered double figures, she appears small for her age — a national organisation with an ambitious program run by two part time directors.

She may be little but each year Playworks offers a giant-sized program designed to shift the ground beneath Australian theatre. In 1995, this program is directed by Clare Grant and Francesca Smith, with administration by Caitlin Newton-Broad.

This year, along with running our national information service, we have written assessments for 50 writers; conducted a series of workshops on Writing the Body with Jenny Kemp (initially in NSW, with spin-offs in ACT and Fremantle), Gail Kelly, Peggy Phelan (visiting from New York University) and Peta Tait; held a public forum on Writing for Radio at the Australian Museum; workshopped the plays of Susie Bromfield (VIC), Noelle Janaczewska and Christine Phillips

(NSW) and Sarah Brill (WA); provided dramaturgical assistance to Sara Hardy (QLD) Anni Finsterer, Melina Marchetta, Matra Robertson and Alana Valentine (NSW). Anni Finsterer's play *Grave Gnomes* was read at the NSW Writers' Centre Spring Fair. This year's showcase of works by four writers will be directed by Sally Richardson and broadcast on ABC Radio. All this and it's only October!

The big event in the 1995 Playworks program is *Playing with Time* our national festival celebrating the decade of Australian women's writing for performance and this accompanying publication.

Playing with Time is a performative event in which 22 writers from around Australia speak their own diary of the decade interrupted by commentaries, questions and performances. This festival presents an all too rare opportunity for Australian women writers to come together. At the International Women Playwrights Conference in Adelaide last year, amongst the excitement of the international guests was the pleasure of meeting Australian women writers for the first time. We hope that fortuitous meetings here will have further spin-offs.

Another pleasure of the Conference was meeting UK writer Deborah Levy who we have now invited back to work with ten Australian women artists on a new version of her *The B File*. Deborah's presence provides a focus for the work of a growing number of Australian women writers working with ideas of identity and language. We're also pleased to have been able to organise in collaboration with Metro Arts, The Performance Space, La Mama and the VCA, for Deborah Levy to conduct workshops in Brisbane and Melbourne.

As with the *Playing with Time* Festival, this survey presents an account of the working lives of writers for theatre and performance in this country along with analysis and projection. It is a snapshot of the scene as we saw it at 5.00 pm September 29 1995 the time we had to say "no more". Though detailed it is by no means the full picture. The findings compiled from the responses of the 90 writers and 111 performing arts companies to our national survey will provide the basis of a database to which we hope the community of women writers, theatre and performance workers will continually contribute, providing us with a constantly evolving picture.

Happy birthday Playworks and many happy returns to all those who have through their involvement in its first decade contributed to the growth of all Australian women's writing for theatre and performance in the next decade.

contents

Definitions of categories used in the text

Large Mainstream: denotes prestigious big budget theatre produced either by subsidised state theatre companies or occasionally their commercial equivalents. Producing largely conventional plays with occasional innovation and some support of Australian playwrights (Sewell, Nowra, Rayson, Williamson). This group includes Melbourne's Playbox and Perth's Black Swan, both now members of the Australia Council's Major Organisations Board.

Small Mainstream includes a range of work from relatively small to quite large overall activity. Medium sized companies include Sydney's Griffin and Brisbane's La Boite. This group also includes regional theatre companies. Work ranges from conventional to innovative. They often share actors, writers and directors with the Large Mainstream.

Community, Youth, Theatre for Young People, and Puppet Theatre: These are usually small companies best known for group devised works and offering many challenges to Australian playwrights. Their audiences include particular communities or schools, but they also reach mainstream audiences with adult and touring works (such as, in the area of puppet theatre, Melbourne's Handspan, Canberra's Company Skylark and Hobart's Terrapin). Through arts festivals, youth theatre companies (Canberra Youth Theatre) and theatres for young people (Adelaide's Magpie) can reach a wider audience. Youth Theatre Companies offer young people experience in devising works, increasingly in arts centres that offer a wide range of collaborative possibilities — dance, visual arts, techno-arts etc.

Contemporary Performance companies and individual artists work at the intersections of theatre, dance, performance art and the new technologies with a strong emphasis on the body, creative processes, performance-audience relations and cultural theories. The artists are often multi-skilled (writer-performers, director-designers etc.) A common role for writers in this area is to provide text or scenario as opposed to script or to work collaboratively or as dramaturgs. This area opens up many new opportunities for writers to explore new ways of writing for performance. Companies include for example Sydney's Sidetrack, Open City, Entr'acte; Canberra's Splinters, Partyline, the work of Lyndal Jones and Peter King (Victoria), Adelaide's Mad Love. Centres such as Sydney's Performance Space, Artspace, Perth's PICA, Adelaide's Experimental Art Foundation and Brisbane's Metro Arts and IMA showcase this work. Some of the work is also from time to time strongly evident in physical theatre companies (like Legs on the Wall) and the indigenous performance company Kooemba Jdarra, as well as in theatres for young people. At a time when much work entails cross art form, multimedia and hybridisation, all of these categories are fluid.

o n e

looking back

Women writers have always been a force in Australia's performing arts. Currency Press publisher, Katharine Brisbane wrote to Playworks:

> *Women have historically had a particular importance in influencing the direction of theatre in Australia. The forward-looking amateur theatre from the 20s to the 50s in Australia was dominated by spirited women who, frustrated by the limitations of the imperialist J. C. Williamson's organisation, set up their own theatres. A high proportion of the playwrights of that period were women, including Katharine Susannah Prichard and Betty Roland, Henrietta Drake-Brockman, Catherine Shepherd, Catherine Duncan, Dymphna Cusack, Dulcie Deamer, Mona Brand and Oriel Gray.*

Director of the Australian National Playwrights Centre, May-Brit Akerholt, points to the relative lack of attention paid to these precursors.

> *But it's interesting to note that Mona Brand, Oriel Gray, Katharine Susannah Prichard and others were among the most active playwrights in the 40s and 50s - and often produced too. They didn't become part of our classic repertoire, however - why? Because they were women? Did Alan Seymour, Ray Lawler et al succeed just because they were men? There are many questions we need to ask and explore.*

Brisbane suggests that the rise of the Australia Council from 1968 made radical changes to the structure of the theatre profession, breaking up many of the pro/am companies headed by women. Akerholt reminds us that when a new surge of energy occurred in Australian theatre, women were not represented in large numbers:

> *Although there are names such as Dorothy Hewett, Alma de Groen and others, the real burst of Australian drama happening in the seventies was dominated by male playwrights. However, we have to acknowledge, I think, that fewer women than men were writing for the stage at that time, we can't just blame a male-oriented system. I also think it's important to explore the very complex reasons for the small percentage of women actively writing for theatre in the past; I don't believe it's as simple as saying they just weren't given the opportunities. The fact is, there were fewer women out there with excellent plays and with the necessary skills to get to the top.*

Yet Katharine Brisbane notes that Playworks had important precursors:

Probably the first feminist group was that within the Australian Performing Group, who produced Betty Can Jump *in 1972, a satire aimed at directing attention to the poor roles for women provided by male writers.*

A major push came in 1981 when Chris Westwood and others at the Nimrod Theatre organised the Women Directors' Workshop and Women and Theatre Project, to develop playwrights, directors and female roles. The early work was largely polemical but it served the purpose of raising public consciousness and in the years that followed drew responses in better roles, in the development of women directors and playwrights and a positive discrimination being shown by the Australia Council boards and theatre managements. Feminist groups sprang up in all states. Today the best known is probably Vitalstatistix, founded in Adelaide in 1984.

Groups such as these, and Playworks itself, have developed in response to wider understanding of some of the issues facing women in the arts.

Government initiatives

To foster the cultural development of the nation and encourage the artistic expression of all individuals, the Australia Council has initiated affirmative action strategies to eliminate discrimination against, and to increase opportunities for, women working in the arts.

A 1990 survey by the Australia Council showed that more women than men think the arts have general social value, 59% believing everyone benefited from increased expenditure on the arts, not just an 'arty group'. Women are well represented in audiences. Nationally women outstrip men in attendances at all arts venues surveyed by the Australian Bureau of Statistics in its 1992 survey of Australians' leisure activities. Andrea Hull has pointed out that:

...arts in the community were once regarded as 'women's work'. It was women throughout Australia who worked for, raised money for, organised for arts activities.[1]

Women are committed to training in the arts. Girls are major participants in arts training at school and at tertiary level.[2] This does not mean women automatically then become creative artists, particularly with the increasing professionalisation of the arts and cultural industries. However, there are signs that women are becoming more committed to becoming active creators: between 1983 and 1993 women identifying themselves as artists grew from 37% of all Australian artists to about 50%.[3] Such equity in numbers has only recently emerged. It has followed a number or reports which demonstrate that women suffered disadvantage in the arts and cultural industries.

A Question of Equity

The 1982 NSW Women and Arts Festival, which celebrated women's contribution to the arts across all fields, provided an important impetus to an investigation of women's involvement. As part of the Festival, the Australia Council initiated a research project looking at needs and problems of women artists, through analysis of statistics and focus group interviews. Its 1983 report, the first in Australia on women in the arts, looked at rates of participation, levels of employment and income and showed considerable evidence of discrimination against women. Women worked in the least powerful positions in arts organisations, and were not as well represented in key creative or decision-making positions. They clustered in the least prestigious artistic fields. Women did not earn as much as men, and received fewer and smaller grants from the Australia Council. They also experienced specific gender-related obstacles to their career path development (in particular absence of childcare).[4]

In 1984, as a result of the report, the Australia Council formulated a Strategy for Action including getting women on boards and improving their employment opportunities in major client organisations. As well, the Council also introduced strategies aimed at increasing the number of individual women applying for grants and receiving funding. Childcare expenses were included as a legitimate project expense.

The Australia Council continues to monitor grants to assess whether women are receiving a reasonable proportion. It also raises broader questions about the position of women as practitioners through all its areas of activity.

Major Australia Council research projects have focused on the economic position of artists and include women in their considerations; they identify the persistence of subtle disadvantage and lower income for women artists.[5] The 1994 report notes the position of women has slightly improved; it still however, shows that women spend the same amount of hours as men, in both arts and non-arts work, but earn less in both areas, and that women are more likely to report problems with childcare responsibilities. The Australia Council has also continued to be a major funder of specific research projects on the situation and status of women in the arts, including research into childcare needs and studies of the music industry and visual arts and craft workers.[6]

A pilot study of women in the performing and visual arts in Western Australia was undertaken in 1991.[7] The study involved interviews with 24 women in performing and visual arts and analysis of data from companies and venues for that year. In the area of theatre, Playworks' major concern, the study investigated nine theatre companies together with five professional theatre groups appearing in Artrage, a fringe arts festival. It found that there was considerable lack of opportunity for women. It was found that most key creative or decision-making positions were filled by men, except the position of stage manager, which the researchers suggest is a more supportive role. Women fared better in small companies where one artistic director and two general managers were female. Women as writers of plays, from a study of grant applications and subscription brochures, were in the minority. Overall, forty five works were produced; of these only ten (22%) were written by women alone; a further seven (16%) were written by women and men together and the majority, twenty eight (62%) were written by men. Men directed thirty of the works, women only twelve and two were jointly directed. Only three dramaturgs were used overall, all male. Works directed by women were less likely to have mainstage productions; only 25% were in the larger theatre spaces. A disproportionate amount of work written by women was performed in schools. In terms of the performance opportunities presented in these works, only 40% were for female actors.

Seven theatre professionals were interviewed, five artists and two managers. Interview data indicated that more works by women playwrights would create better female roles. Others made the point that plays written by women were seen as less important and less commercial. It was also suggested that women writers had a different approach to content. The one playwright interviewed strongly argued for the importance of "women's stories".

> *Men want theatre that is controversial and confronting whereas theatre can be about resolution and celebration. (Men's) dramatic writing often has a protagonist who acts and who changes behaviour and who promotes conflict, but women's lives are often about diffusing conflict and about being reactive.*

She emphasised the importance of female artistic directors for women's plays:

> *There is a tendency for male artistic directors to sentimentalise women; they don't want to present women as dangerous — except within the parameters they accept as dangerous such as the whore or castrating mother.*

She noted that when women were represented as diffusing conflict,

> *...male directors want to portray them as victims whereas women can recognise these characters as powerful women doing small psychological things, not big action.*

Exploring new ways of analysing women's participation

Gillian Swanson of Griffith University's Institute for Cultural Policy Studies argues that there are problems with equity analyses which evaluate women's performance against that of men, look at their participation in terms of disadvantage and produce recommendations for ameliorative measures which even up the balance. Unfortunately, these leave the benchmarks in place, not questioning whether these are the most appropriate measures for women's participation.

Swanson was team leader for an as yet unpublished confidential survey on women in the arts and cultural industries commissioned by the Australia Council and Arts Queensland in 1994. Rather than undertaking only an equity analysis, based on evidence of discrimination, lack of acceptance, bias and gender imbalance, she proposed an industry analysis which looked at the distinctive features of the arts and cultural industries.

The report shows that women working in the arts possess a high level of professional qualifications, experience and multiple skills; demonstrate high levels of career mobility; earn low incomes; and lack confidence in applying for government funding. Women identify marketing skills as important. A significant proportion of women self-define as cross-arts, or practise in more than one discipline, for example, musicians, film-makers or performance artists who also write. Women practitioners are also likely to be involved in some proportion of collective practice and collaborative work. Most of these also practice individually.

Writers interviewed, including writers for other genres such as fiction, tend to be self-employed and work at home (83% of writers). Writers earn very little: 69% of them earn under $5000. Women writers also have limited confidence in applying for government funding (only 43% of writers do, whereas 66% of theatre workers do and 65% of film makers).[8]

A more detailed analysis of an industry, *What Do I Wear in a Hurricane?*, gives a picture of trends and career patterns in film, television and radio. Its recommendations focus on specific areas (such as camera-work) and design measures to improve women's options according to skill base and recruitment. It addresses questions of training and professional development. Report authors Cox and Laura do not abandon the equity model arguing, for example, for training quotas. Their overall push, however, is a strategy which aims at "changing the operations of the industry to make them both more efficient and able to deal with gender diversity", while also outlining measures "to assist women to use and promote the skills they have most effectively" and develop management practices "to give women extra training and experience." [9]

They acknowledge that writers are in an influential position, 'the key to creative input into characters, plots and issues,' and quote a Paul Byrnes' *Sydney Morning Herald* review of *The Last Days of Chez Nous*.

> *Defining who we are is something Australian films rarely attempt, at least in a critical way. Our films tend to think of Australian-ness only in masculine and positive terms.* Chez Nous *is different. Here is a definition of mostly Australian life in female terms and the effect is jolting - at least it was for me. Everything about novelist and scriptwriter Helen Garner's characters was familiar but I wasn't expecting to see them on an Australian screen. Women like these have been noticeably absent from our films.*

Cox and Laura note that in a previous survey in 1985/6, women were 18% of writers in feature films, but in 1993 they were 27%. They propose to deal with this continuing shortfall by establishing a mentors program for creative women and a special workshop organised by the AFC and the AFTRS for women screen/script writers to explore ways and means of increasing their role on major projects.

Women in the Performing Arts

In attempting to consider the characteristics of performing arts as an industry sector, one of the most useful analyses is Peta Tait's *Converging Realities: Feminism in Australian Theatre*, Currency Press/Artmoves, 1994. This book is important for our purposes in that Tait is concerned with feminist involvement and reconstruction in performing arts.

She argues that theatre is a social space in which the "performative nature of cultural and individual identity" is explored. Her book powerfully shows how recent women practitioners of theatre and performance in Australia have enlarged the scope of existing theatrical forms. They use a diversity of writing forms, physical styles, spaces and structures to express female experiences. The theatre practices she describes subvert existing theatrical forms and create new ones, such as women's circus which Tait identifies as a radical Australian innovation which has been extended by feminist practitioners.

While this Playworks project is interested in exploring not just feminist work, but work by all women writing for performance, Tait's argument is important in that it reminds us it is not enough to identify disadvantage for women in the fact that women may not be represented in equal numbers on the main stages of theatre companies. Instead, it is important to look at all these questions in the context of genres, form, political commitment and venues chosen. Many women elect to work outside these constraints. The writers chosen for this survey reflect the diversity of women's contribution to performing arts.

t w o

Write Your Own Bloody Play!

*In Canberra about 1981 at a Playwrights Conference, [ANPC], I was
forever commenting on and criticising the dearth of good roles for women
in the plays; finally a man in the audience (well-known actor/director)
yelled at me: "Well, write your own bloody play!!" So I did.*

Suzanne Spunner

The responses to the Playworks survey show that women in Australia have
indeed been writing their own "bloody plays", or their own works for community
groups, theatre in education, physical theatre, young people's theatre and
experimental performance. The women responding to the Playworks survey
demonstrate the diversity of women writing for performance in Australia.

Altogether 90 women writers answered the survey. We approached women
writers who defined themselves as professional and, apart from a couple who
were just beginning writers, all had had works performed or in major
development. This section is based on their words, their questions, their debates.
We have drawn freely from their surveys and have arranged the sections so that a
discussion between different views emerges. Most writers were happy to be
quoted when asked for permission, but three requested anonymity, and some
wished particular responses not to be credited.

The following figures are derived from the responses of 80 women writing for
performance in Australia, the final ten arrived too late for inclusion in the tables.
We tabulated their years of writing, their output, their success gaining
production and whether they had an agent.

Figure 1 shows the number of years that our respondents had been writing.
Thirteen had been writing for over twenty years, one of them for more than thirty.
Thirty additional respondents had been writing for between ten and twenty years
and thirty seven for less than ten years. As can be seen from Figure 1, however,
the majority, 57%, have been writing for between five and fifteen years.

Considering the length of time that the women had been writing, Playworks was
concerned to note how few had agents. Of the eighty responses analysed, only
twenty-five had an agent and in three of those cases women, in fact, relied on a
manager or a theatre company. It should also be pointed out that a number of the
women worked also as performers and their agents had initially represented them
as such.

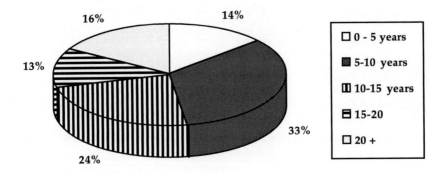

Figure 1: Women writers: number of years writing

Fifty-five of the writers had no agent, although some of these were writers of long experience and many productions. Figure 2 shows that in fact there is little overall difference between the two groups, except in the proportion of written works which have been produced. Women with agents have been writing for an average of eleven years; women without agents for an average of ten (in fact nine of them had been writing for over twenty years). Women with agents had written over 150 works, 94% of which had been produced. Women without agents had written 360 works, 82% of which had been produced. In some cases women had multiple productions of one work - these have been counted as one production.

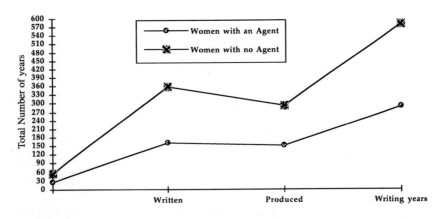

Figure 2: Writers, writers with agents, number of productions and number years writing

Playworks was able to undertake a detailed statistical analysis of the first thirty-four writers who responded. The majority (twenty-two) developed full-length works for the stage or musical theatre. A significant group, however, developed work which they defined as experimental or performative. Eight had written work in addition for TIE or youth theatre, eight for radio, seven for community theatre. It should be noted that none of these specialised in these areas, but moved between genres. Twelve of the women had written collaboratively; most of these also wrote individually. Half of the writers indicated that they had written works which had been developed through to a reading workshop phase, but had as yet not been performed. All of these had other works produced.

Statistics are however not the main aim of this survey. It has given us an opportunity to hear the actual voices and opinions of 90 contemporary Australian women writers. Let us hear them:

A double-edged sword

A theme that emerges from many respondents is the double-edged nature of being a woman writing for theatre. As Jenny Kemp writes:

Perhaps it is both an advantage and a disadvantage to be a member of a minority/marginal group — which allows for both a sense of real freedom/anarchy as it simultaneously disempowers and disables. But I believe this to be true of anyone trying to work in new ways, whatever the gender.

Some women have found that their careers are nurtured by the new policies of theatre managements and funding bodies. The reasons for an increased commitment to women writers include a commitment to equity, a recognition of the value of women's writing and demand from audiences to see more of it. Other respondents however report a more problematic relationship with theatre companies or with a sense of tokenism.

Many of the women responding point to the differences in the content of women's work in terms of characters, themes and structures. Some have found that their subject matter is sometimes threatening to more traditional companies. Many find excitement in the possibilities of experimentation and new forms outside the conventional structure of the 'well made play'.

Some women are actively developing their own work and working with others to produce it. Some are commissioned again and again by theatre in education and community theatre companies, but, while stressing that they value this work highly, feel that the very preponderance of women in the field may lead to its being undervalued. Others express concern at being trapped in development.

There are practical difficulties raised which do relate to gender, in particular child-care and family responsibilities which affect a number of women writers at points in their life cycle, and which delay their ability to develop a cohesive career.

Many of the issues raised by writers are not gender specific. There are problems in the relationships between directors and writers; writers are frustrated by the time taken to receive assessments of their work. The existence of networks for writers is seen as a positive benefit in providing support for writers. There is also evidence among successful playwrights of the growing attraction of writing for film and television.

Respondents raise issues not only of equity in career opportunities, but of the intimate relationship between their work as women playwrights/performers and their discovery/forging of identity. It's a strong thread that connects the writer and her work, and many respondents tell stories of their fight to hold onto that thread, and save themselves and their work from distortion, neglect or abuse. Although there is no way for our survey to calculate whether threads frayed under pressure, or to count the number of lost works, lost writers, we can celebrate with the women writers who have responded their efforts to weave new patterns in Australian theatre and performance.

Dear Playworks

I have been writing for performance for over twenty years. My first attempts as an emerging playwright were produced in 1977, although I had contributed to group devised work for many years prior to that date.

I was an 'actress' whose life was severely impacted by the women's movement, and for better or for worse, I remain committed to feminism. I began to write to place women centre stage, to create roles where they were seen as the subject not the object of a play.

In the early years of my development I believed myself to be part of the mainstream but experienced the sense of being 'other', not quite a real person. I was acutely aware that my view of the world was uniquely mine and reflected a female perspective in all things political, social and philosophical.

And from this perspective I saw that male writers and their world view was the first option. Women appeared lower down on the list until it was realised there was an audience out there wanting to hear what women had to say.

The label 'woman writer' is a double-edged sword. It can clear the way, cut you loose, and stab you in the back. It is a weapon and a wand.

The struggle has been two-fold. A writer in search of craft. A woman in search of recognition. Recognition of herself.

Hilary Beaton

These are exciting times

There is a sense of energy and expectancy among women writers for performance ·— a sense that women have gained in skill, that much work is flourishing already, and that much more is on the way.

Many respondents report eager audiences who want to hear what women have to say and want to see performances that explore women's experience and history.

In 1994-95 four new works by Queensland writers premiered to enthusiastic response - Hilary Beaton's *No Strings Attached*, Elaine Acworth's *Composing Venus*, Jill Shearer's *The Family* and Fawnia Mountford's performance work, *Tramp-o-line*.

Successful bilingual works from Australia include Noelle Janaczewska's *The History of Water* opening this month in Ottawa and Anna Broinowski's *The Gap* which has recently toured Japan.

Margaret Kirby reports that when her play, *My Body. My Blood*, was produced at St Paul's Cathedral Chapter House, Melbourne, audience comments included:

> *...very moved...made me think...I cried — want to see it again...want to bring my mother...extraordinary...didn't expect it to be relevant to me...*

All the aforementioned works will be published by Currency Press this year.

Meanwhile Katherine Thomson's *Diving for Pearls* has entered the 'Australian classic' category with three productions around Australia this year.

Lyn Coleman, who directed Peta Murray's play, *Wallflowering* for The Adelaide University Theatre Guild and is taking the production to the 1995 Melbourne Fringe, comments that the play has always had excellent notices and tumultuous audience response.

Melbourne's Jenny Kemp's *The Black Sequinned Dress* has been commissioned by Barrie Kosky for the 1996 Adelaide Festival.

Ruth Conley-Watson, a cabaret and comedy writer/performer notes significant changes in audience attitudes towards work with a women's perspective:

> *When I first performed 'female' comedy at The Last Laugh in the early eighties, audiences were stunned. In the nineties, female comediennes are writing and performing their work to educated, responsive audiences (mostly!).*

Of the six plays chosen by French producers for the *Sydney Plays Paris Exchange* with the STC this year, the four plays by women (Karin Mainwaring, Hilary Bell, Elaine Acworth and Hannie Rayson) were among the most enthusiastically received at the Comedie Francaise.

I think I've been lucky

There has been in the past ten years a strong campaign for equity, encouraged, among others, by the Australia Council. A number of respondents, still a minority, report that their careers are enhanced by recent policies of theatre managements. Hannie Rayson, whose plays are highly acclaimed and regularly performed in major theatres, writes:

> Over the past decade the appetite for a female vision in the theatre has developed from management and audiences alike. This has bolstered my career significantly. Managements have learned that a large proportion of audiences are women.

> I'm not sure whether this is gender related but I feel I have been very nurtured as a playwright. Artistic managements (Playbox, Sydney Theatre Company, Queensland Theatre Company) actively wanted women playwrights to develop and mature as writers.

Similarly, Beatrix Christian welcomes writing during a period of support from funding bodies and companies:

> I think I've been very lucky. Everything I've written has been produced, so the subject matter's getting by the censors. If anything there's been a slight advantage in being a woman in terms of funding from the Australia Council.

Karin Mainwaring acknowledges:

> I am able to generally take advantage of the advances that feminism has worked for. In this sense I am most definitely advantaged.

Debra Oswald observes:

> Sometimes being a woman is an advantage when companies and other organisations want to be seen to include a requisite number of women. In those cases, women writers get a few extra points.

Elizabeth Spencer makes a similar point without Debra's trace of cynicism:

> There is more federal and state funding available for women writers who deal with women's issues, and much more support for those issues being voiced.

For emerging writers there is an exciting optimism about writing for performance. Sharon Guest has been writing for four years and notes that:

> There appear to be more avenues to encourage women writers e.g. competitions specifically for women writers.

Christine Gillespie says:

You do hear around the traps that theatre directors are looking for 'good'
plays by women.

Similarly Anna North, with one play showcased, points out that although a 'boy's
club' still operates,

...there is a huge market for pertinent writing by young women.

Jenny Swain concurs:

Sometimes I think that being a woman writing for performance and also
specialising in musical theatre, well, it can't help but be a 'growth
industry'.

Mardi McConnochie also celebrates the potential:

As a young woman I find myself eminently fundable, since women and
youth are both priority areas. The networks of support that have been
made available to me have given me all sorts of opportunities to develop
my skills both as writer and dramaturg, and to get my work on the stage,
and seeing your work performed is what it's all about.

The backlash has come so quickly

Attempts to achieve equal opportunity for women are still small steps compared
to their historic disadvantage. A number of respondents observe that there are
problems in the theatre that face male as well as female playwrights. "However,"
writes one respondent, "theatre companies are still doing more plays by men, and
men are in the majority as artistic directors." Some writers caution against
acceptance of an assumption that women have been well treated and are now
equal.

Mardi McConnochie points out:

It has not escaped my attention that in the 1995 Sydney Theatre Company
subscription season there is only one play by a woman; at Belvoir Street
Theatre there are no plays by women; Griffin's season is not a whole lot
better. There are so few roles for women performers on the mainstages of
Sydney that they can all be adequately covered by five performers.

One respondent observed that there is a backlash against feminism, and that it's
now considered "out of date".

Patricia Cornelius, a writer for performance, perceives that compared with men,
women lack personal and professional support for their work. She challenges the

perception that special advantages are given to women writers:

> *I have arguments all the time about how much more funding, more of everything we (are alleged to) receive!*

This point is strongly made by Darwin writer Venetia Gillot; what is seen as a window of opportunity for women who have experienced historic discrimination may be resented by others and rapidly slammed shut.

> *For so long women of colour found the white middle class feminists talked about woman as a class, and assumed they were speaking for all, and didn't acknowledge differences of culture and class. It was not sitting right for me. I have to speak from my voice. There is commonality but lots of differences...There's the whole issue of class, race and poverty — that's the bottom line — the whole thing of finding your voice. Only now is space being made for women of colour. Suddenly we've been given a voice, but the backlash has come so quickly — lack of support, refusing to engage in the dialogue, people shutting down, "Oh gosh, you have to be ethnic now to get a grant." Or, "You're only being asked because of your ethnicity." Not even said out loud, just implied. It's hard for traditional feminists feeling they are under attack. Why are you feeling so threatened? Call it what it is, this is racism.*

Paula Abood agrees:

> *Despite the rather monotonous views of the 'disaffected' that one is more likely to be successful in terms of funding if you are female and from a non-English speaking background, the statistics, the reality do not back up this view.*

That I worry about tokenism is probably my own insecurity

Some of the complexities of being a member of a group apparently targeted for positive discrimination are voiced by Jodi Gallagher:

> *The sense that any critical reception of my work — from companies and reviewers — is conditioned by the fact that I'm a female playwright is, in a sense, both a blessing and a curse. For example my play* Banshee *was recently included in a series of readings,* Playwrights Raw, *at the Playbox — I submitted it when a friend told me that they were specifically looking for women playwrights. The fact the company is aware of an equitable programming policy is undoubtedly good, and in this case being female was an advantage.*

> *The fact that I worry about tokenism is probably my own insecurity, or maybe not — I can't tell. At the same time, the apparently*

'confrontational' nature of my subject matter makes it both easier and more difficult. It's made more confrontational by the fact that I'm a woman writing it — and I enjoy that, I want it to hit hard. But at the same time, should it hit harder because I'm a woman? Or not?

Sue-Anne Post points out that women are asked to prove more.

Wish I had a buck for every time I've heard "Yeah, pretty funny ... for a sheila/chick/girl".

There's no room for failure, and you have to be twice as funny. The boys have so much more leeway for failure, and dud performances. Other boys will make sure they still get work. Women get no such support.

Jenny Kemp believes women face specific obstacles:

Women are basically not presumed to be capable — they must prove and prove and prove again their capabilities to gain credibility.

Claire Haywood observes that:

The directors who program plays for companies are not attuned to the issues that women audiences would respond to and therefore favour male writing. I think one has to work harder to establish credibility.

Anna Broinowski also indicates that women's achievements may not be given due recognition.

The Gap — my first play — was also the first Australian play (as opposed to dance work or performance piece) ever to tour to Japan. Had I been a young male, I wonder whether the project would have been more fully recognised as the pioneering cross-cultural coup that it was.

Catherine Zimdahl highlights another problem, the expectations placed on a woman writer.

If a director or producer is looking specifically for a woman writer then I have more chance of a job. This however sometimes comes with the expectation to be the authoritative 'voice of woman'.

Craftsmen first, women second

Elaine Acworth comments that the process of becoming a writer goes in a series of stages.

To begin you learn to value the work. You're scrupulous in your attention to critics, dramaturgs, the workshop process, the opinions of those select readers it's taken some years to find, because the focus is on making a better play. It's on the play.

The next stage (the one I'm in) is to value yourself as maker, helmsman, juggler, puzzle solver, channel, leaper in the dark, whatever. I realise that I've been looking at my process more and more in the last twelve months understanding it as my active thing, not an Act of God.

The third stage is appreciating how you work and are understood by the rest of the world. That's a bit of a doozy: to be confronted with the notion that you require a public persona, especially when you're doing stage two. They're the ones I've seen so far. There may be more. If so, I'm thankful you generally don't get to see the whole road ahead, just the next few steps are enough for me at the moment.

Some writers wish to be recognised for their work, not because of their gender. Tobsha Learner sees this as a slow evolution:

There will not be a revolution but an achingly slow osmosis from the time we are defined as women playwrights to the time we are defined as craftsmen (sic) first, women second.

Suzanne Hawley is optimistic:

I believe if somebody, anybody writes a good script, then somebody will be interested in it. Male or female. I have found no discrimination.

Anna Broinowski perceives:

Danger still exists of a play being marginalised as 'women's writing' simply because the author is female. This is particularly so with 'fringe' work. We need to challenge/reshape the dominant paradigm so that 'art' takes precedence over 'gender'

It's not that they keep you out on purpose

More than one respondent uses the word 'subtle' to describe the obstacles women face compared with men. Playwright, performer and producer Margaret Fischer, who has been working since 1984 with Vitalstatistix, a women's theatre company she co-founded, writes:

At first I was doing group devised work and felt competitive pressure from men in a subtle sense. I formed a women's theatre company in 1984 so my own and other women's work would be produced.

Margaret reports over the past ten years consistently lower grant levels for Vitalstatistix compared with mixed gender companies.

Other women writers argue that they still require support, particularly in certain work contexts. Beatrix Christian speaks about her relationship with the Sydney Theatre Company:

I think that some 'special treatment' is crucial for women because, from my experience as a writer in residence at the Sydney Theatre Company, there's definitely a support network that exists and, in the sort of work that I do, fairly straightforward, narrative drama, there aren't many women.

There's a group of male writers who are fairly well established, there's an audience following for them, a certain sense of security for the theatre companies that, if they put on their work, there'll be an audience for it.

At the State Theatre Company level there are very few women to guide you. That's how it's been historically. It's not that they keep you out on purpose. It's an inadvertent thing. Therefore any effort to turn around the imbalance is very important, because it's hard to do that from the inside.

Lois Achimovich writes:

I believe the field is still dominated by men but I have received encouragement from both men and women in my own development.

Playwright Julie Janson's words reveal a tension between expectations stirred by the perception of increased opportunity, and the reality:

I think women are being given a good chance to succeed in theatre, but the statistics on how many women's plays are produced are depressing. It's better than it was!

The statistics reviewed later in this report show that there are still fewer works by women produced and other research demonstrates that women writers for performance generally earn less than males in their field. This imbalance seems to persist despite perceptions of increased opportunities for women, increasing interest in women's work from audiences and reviewers. Why?

There is no precedent

One of the major problems women identified was working without a tradition of female writing. For playwright Mardi McConnochie the credibility of women playwrights suffers from a lack of example:

Australian mainstream theatre culture is unnecessarily fixated on the blokey theatre of the 1970s, ignoring the long (buried, denied, unpublished) history of women's writing for performance which reaches well back into the colonial period. Unfortunately you have to be a scholar to know about that, and it means that you have nothing to use as evidence if you are trying to defend the notion of women's writing. It would be nice to have major figures to point to, to be able to say: There's a woman writer; she's important and I am too. We have Dorothy Hewett, whose work is infrequently performed and regarded as difficult; Katherine Susannah Prichard, museum theatre despite (or perhaps because of) its being taught on university English courses; more recently, Alma de Groen, Katherine Thomson, Hannie Rayson, a few others.

This lack of a canon results in what feminist scholars have called "the anxiety of influence". The life and depth and excitement of theatre comes, in the literary sense, from an engagement with past practices, ideas, forms, styles, stories, through re-writing or re-discovering or exploding what has come before. For those of us who believe that women's writing is not the same as men's, we have nothing much to draw on — certainly no large body of cultural forms/knowledge. There is a great gap from Aphra Behn to the 20th century. This literary anxiety, the product of repressive and exclusive critical practices, is manifest in a frustrating sense of isolation.

This gap is also identified by Jennifer Compton who despite her 27 years of professional experience, and many successful stage and radio plays sees all writing as a continuing struggle, a search:

Self doubt. Lashings of self doubt. There is no precedent. No famous women playwrights in history. No path. If you want to be a novelist you look to Jane Austen and Charlotte Bronte. If you want to be a poet you look to Sappho. If you want to be a playwright, whom do you look to? People always say, there's Aphra Behn ... Sometimes I feel really worried, we'll all get stoned in the square for wanting to be female playwrights.

Alana Valentine has been profoundly influenced by her perception of the treatment received by other women writing for the mainstage in Australia. She writes:

Women writers' presence has been both erratic and unsustained. All writers, women included, succeed if they can communicate in the form and content expectations of a significantly male hierarchy in the theatre industry. Ultimately, they have trouble at mid-career and beyond in trying to get their work produced or re-produced.

Male culture decides what's epic

The absence of a female canon has significant results in the valuing of women's voice. For many respondents, the main power to define what is good or bad writing for the stage is perceived to be in the hands of predominantly male directors who operate within a cultural tradition that regards male stories, styles, forms and themes as central and, indeed, essential for successful drama, and for box-office receipts.

Sally Richardson detects:

> *An attitude that themes/subjects relating to women/female experience are box office poison. Why is it when you say, "Hey, guys I don't think it's fair", you get treated as a sore loser?*

For Heather Nimmo an important factor is:

> *A male culture which decides what is epic and what is domestic: men with drinking problems are epic, women with drinking problems are domestic.*

Cathy Craigie writes:

> *As an Aboriginal woman it's difficult to get mainstream theatres to be serious about my work. Australian theatre is still very Eurocentric.*

Mardi McConnochie indicates that some of her most cooperative work has been with a young male director friend; but another director told her that:

> *...he was sick to death of seeing plays about middle-aged women and their trivial problems on the mainstages of Sydney, and that it was about time we saw some plays about really important things.*

She also describes in detail an experience at a writing course run by a major institution:

> *Week in and week out the women playwrights in the course fought with the men running the course about the possibility of women's writing that was different from traditional models of writing. We said that women were attracted to different modes of story-telling, different sorts of stories, and had different approaches to structure, etc. They said that there was good writing and bad writing, that they knew what good writing was, and that the stuff we were arguing for was bad writing. Or, being generous, literary but not dramatic. At no point were they willing to acknowledge that a woman writer, a woman director, or a female audience member might be attracted to stories that didn't interest the guys. Stories were interesting to them, or they were not interesting. The course was about learning to write mainstream three-act narrative drama and "if you're not interested in that sort of drama you shouldn't be doing the course". But I am interested in writing that sort of drama and I still found myself arguing constantly, partly in defence of my own work, but more often in support of my fellow students, who were being quite viciously attacked. All in all, it was an ugly and destructive experience...*

It's probably something to do with young women with university degrees talking back to older men without university degrees about something on which the older men are supposed to be authoritative. I continue to tell myself that these sorts of attitudes are isolated examples and emerge out of personality conflicts rather than more deep-seated beliefs about women's writing.

One woman playwright reports that several smaller companies were considering producing her play, but they decided not to because:

...they had to be careful about their audiences this year, and a play with a cast of three women might put people off.

In Suzanne Spunner's words a significant factor is:

Resistance by critics, and men in particular, to fitness of certain subjects for theatre, especially in terms of character, narrative and dramatic conflict.

Margaret Kirby writes that it usually takes a lot longer for women writers to be taken seriously:

The subjects which interest me — relationships, the particularity of home, women's experience, family — are not seen as important in male terms — older men in particular find it difficult to give you authority/credibility. (If you are) writing from a feminist perspective, many men don't know how to read your work.

Playwright Jennifer Bethel makes a similar assessment of the power held by male gatekeepers:

I sometimes think both the subject matter and style are assessed based on male values as to what's relevant, significant, entertaining.

From Western Australia Marlish Glorie writes:

The theatre appears to be dominated by men who don't take women writers seriously.

Everything remains to be said

The very absence of a canon provides many with opportunities. Many women writers savour the chance to tell their stories in a new voice. Beatrix Christian:

If you subscribe to the theory, which I do, that there are only a certain number of stories, then writing them from a woman's perspective gives you an advantage, because they haven't been written from that perspective thousands of times before. Women have a whole treasure trove of stories we haven't told in our way yet.

Therese Radic also welcomes

...a new view of an art form dominated by men and a new view of contemporary life reflected in allegorical usage.

Jennifer Compton rejoices that:

Nothing has been said. Everything remains to be said. I don't feel as if I am writing for myself. I am writing to say the things that haven't been said. I don't feel as if I will ever run out of material.

Sarah Brill finds possible advantage in the fact that there is so much of women's experience still untold in theatre, but sees that 'writing female stories for a society based on male stories' can also be problematic. A script she submitted for Interplay 94 was rejected, then later sought for production by Shopfront who could not find in the chosen plays any that had "sufficiently strong women characters...and thus needed to resort to mine".

One playwright explained that one reason she moved into writing (as well as directing which had been her career for many years) was that she was dissatisfied with the lack of good new plays available and especially written from a woman's point of view. Now, she feels:

...an ease in writing for a perceived gap — i.e. women's history and experience in Australia.

Anna Broinowski similarly finds:

Simply writing through the 'female gaze' in the '90's affords me a peculiarity of insight not yet captured by predominantly male theatricality of the past. Also, good women's roles come naturally!

Dina Panozzo:

I feel as women we still don't figure enough in the larger picture, especially those of us who think we haven't got the structures and emotional safety needed. Interestingly enough, I find this chaotic experience is the very heart of my work as a performance writer.

There are also strong professional and career reasons for supporting women writers. Leila Hayes, for example, writes plays as showcases for her drama students.

In the professional world I'm sure I'd experience more difficulty. As an actress I am acutely aware of the lack of performed works that have been written by women.

A number of respondents speak of qualities in their work that come from their experience as women. Julie Janson comments:

> ...*we have an insight into female consciousness and this experience has only just been allowed to appear in a male dominated theatre world.*

Marlish Glorie believes:

> *Women write for different reasons from men. Women writers bring a great emotional richness to the stage.*

Two respondents went a step further, claiming, like Pauline Hosking:

> ...*a greater ability to write both male and female characters, because as women they can draw on greater insight and emotional knowledge.*

One respondent perceives that:

> *The advantage is women can write interesting female characters — which many male writers cannot.*

Margaret Kirby sees an advantage in the way as a woman she is able to understand human feelings:

> *I understand women better than most men writing for performance do. As well most men I know don't like themselves and don't know what they feel. (I have the) advantage of being outside watching male behaviour lovingly.*

You write hard subjects for a woman

A small proportion of respondents stated that they did not see themselves as writing from a gendered viewpoint, but as writing about human relationships. Anna Lall:

> *As I don't write on women's issues overtly I think perhaps my insights are not dissimilar to any male or female writer who focuses on the intricacies of human relationships.*

Jodi Gallagher, who has been writing for five years, says:

> *Needless to say I've heard the usual stuff from a lot of people — "you write well for a woman", "you write hard subjects for a woman"— but I do the only thing you can with that and dismiss the speaker as a dickhead.*

It is important to note that many critics and audiences rejoice in the broad vision that women writers offer and indicate that they represent a view of both men and women. Playwright Hilary Beaton's *Outside In*, which is set in a women's prison, is praised for its presentation not just of the experience of the women:

It is a fascinating play for its exploration of why women arrive in this situation, and of why, once there, some begin to internalise traditionally 'male' values — and why all human beings find it easier to kick against a system that they know than to face breaking out of it. Most immediately though, it says a great deal about human relationships on a smaller scale brought into focus by the playwright's own production.[10]

Virginia Jane Rose, whose play *Freedom of the Heart* received a Commendation in the Drama category of the 1994 Human Rights Awards, comments:

I don't know that my advantages are necessarily gender-linked. My biggest advantages are: powerful and original imagination; wide experience of and interest in people of all kinds and conditions; good analytical and structural skills; plotting ability with passion for love, hope and justice.

Jenny Swain adds:

When I started writing for performance I was particularly committed to writing for women performers and with a feminist message, but to be heard by a wider audience. So it's not surprising that my material was labelled 'women's cabaret' and 'feminist theatre'. As I've grown, the issues that I want to explore have broadened. I work with men more, too, and although I still have a strongly feminist perspective, my work is not marginalised. Sometimes it seems that if men just perform in your work the labels disappear.

Self = (woman)?

For some respondents, a woman writer who puts female characters centrestage may be at risk of having her work distorted, diminished, denigrated or dismissed as bad writing, because it focuses on women, on the autobiographical or the apparently confessional.

Noëlle Janaczewska is critical of:

...the assumption that women's work is autobiographical (when it is not) and therefore a kind of 'lesser' creation.

Maryanne Lynch notes the same:

(There is a) strong tendency of others to equate work with self = (woman). Caught between the desert and the deep blue sea, I/my work have been categorised as either emotive (viz. you are a handful) or intellectual (viz. you are cold and repressed). I can't help thinking that a male writer wouldn't carry the same imagined baggage of autobiography/history. I suppose I'll face more obstacles when I 'lose my looks'!

Suzanne Spunner recalls the response to the 1982/3 productions of her group - developed performance piece *Not Still Lives* produced by the Home Cooking Company which she and other Melbourne women formed in 1981:

> *Female critics were fulsome in their praise for innovations in form and subject matter. Male critics (in general) hated it. They said it did not reach a 'general public' audience; it appealed to feminists and people interested in Australian Art History.*

Suzanne experienced similarly contrasting responses to *Running up a Dress,* toured by Home Cooking Theatre Company. It had two sell out seasons in Melbourne and a Bathurst Island performance under a mango tree for an audience of Tiwi women who worked at Bima Wear, a women's sewing business. While audiences responded to the subject matter and were excited by the way it was "not like television", male critics deplored a "lack of dramatic conflict".

Paula Williams sees as a self-engendered obstacle:

> *...a non-gutsy, non-confrontational style which is currently unfashionable, as much women's writing now has developed the masculine attack/ cut/thrust approach.*

Annette Rups-Eyland submits herself to:

> *A constant/continuous review and awareness of researching and questioning my own perspective on 'how things are' and 'how things could be'. I and my pieces have been called "indulgent" and "emotional" and my material "more relevant to women than men".*

So what did everyone think of that, apart from disgusting?

For many women writers the struggle to be taken seriously includes a struggle to gain acceptance for content and form which offers a strong challenge to standard perspectives.

Rejection of women's writing because of its content is not a new problem. Alison Lyssa speaks of her unsuccessful attempt in 1985 to get an agent on the strength of her contract with Methuen (UK) for the publication of her play *Pinball.*

> *The play is about a struggle for the soul of a child. It's also about a lesbian custody case. The agent, a woman, handed the script back: "The writing's good, but the subject matter...(pause with eyes averted)...I don't see how anybody could put that on".*

Yet subsidised theatres in two Australian cities already had produced it and it had had a reading in New York.

Alison hasn't yet got an agent, and dines out on that story as a crystallisation of the reasons for her silence as a playwright for a decade, except for the safety of small community theatre projects. It's a silence she is now changing, having recently written a new play, *Where There's a Will*. Alison believes that:

> *It's impossible to measure the effects of a censorship policy that officially pretends it doesn't exist, but unofficially denies opportunities to those who transgress it.*

Sandra Shotlander who describes herself as writing as a woman, as a feminist and as a lesbian, reports the response when she sought a mainstage production for one of her plays:

> *Playbox's rejection of* Is That You Nancy? *is very telling: "It has sharp humour and is well written, but for a Playbox audience would mainly have 'curiosity' value...for those of like persuasion, but not of broad appeal."[11]*

The responses to Sandra's play *Angels of Power* illustrate how content that challenges traditional gender and family roles can be sharply polarising. Under the headline "The joke's on us, fellas", reviewer Bob Crimeen assured any male theatre goer that "he faces a tough night's theatre. Ms Shotlander's pro-feminist writings stir female passions and shred male consciences". While warning the men he describes the response of the predominantly female audience on opening night as "one of the most prolonged ovations accorded a play in Melbourne for a long time".

Sandra indicated that the play's anonymous assessor for the Performing Arts Board of the Australia Council and the reviewer for *The Age*, Leonard Radic, dramatically diverged in their views on its content, dialogue, structure and relevance, understandable for a play with a challenging content. For example, the assessor described it as "a simple political statement that men are manipulators and we would be better off with a matriarchy". Radic on the other hand described it on production as an " imaginative satire on the uses and abuses of power by male authority figures".

As a young playwright Mardi McConnochie was selected for two successive Young Playwrights' Conferences, the 1988 international one, and the 1989 national one. She saw even then an ongoing tension about women's writing versus men's writing.

> *Directors were urging us girls to write about women's experiences, to be bolder, tougher, more daring; but I felt fairly certain at the time that the plays by women which were actually being selected were not the bold, tough and daring ones. I felt that there was a taste being exhibited by the people choosing the delegates for cosy, domestic Neighbours-style drama*

by girls, warm social or romantic comedies. It appeared to me that plays by women were being chosen on the basis of technical skill and ability to control form, rather than the excitement of the ideas or quality of imagination. Which is fair enough, I suppose. At the 1989 conference, I got in on the strength of an old play but actually took a new and unseen one along to the conference. It was a loud, messy affair to do with lesbian vampires, revenge and television and I thought it was cool. After it was read by the actors the person running the conference got up and said, "So what did everyone think of that, apart from disgusting?" He said afterwards he was joking, but as a self-righteous 18 year old I didn't think it sounded like a joke. I thought at the time I would never have got to the conference if I'd submitted that play.

My aim is transgressive writing

While the work of women writers generally is seen by some to be achieving a greater, and much needed recognition, a number of respondents expressed the view that there is not a ready acceptance of feminist and/or lesbian writing.

Alana Valentine is one of several respondents remarking that there can be a gender-based difference in what companies consider acceptable content for a play, particularly in those relating to sexuality.

... while plays about male sexuality, particularly male homosexuality, have moved from transgressive fringe theatre to mainstage status there does not seem to have been a similar movement of plays about women's sexuality.

There is a resounding silence from the Australian mainstages about issues of female sexuality, particularly female homosexuality. I would go so far as to say that this kind of work has, with some brave exceptions, been discriminated against by mainstage companies.

As another woman playwright puts it:

Gay men seem to get their work on gay relationships accepted more easily than plays about lesbians as opposed to 'women's friendships'.

Alana Valentine names the effort needed to overcome being pressed into shape by those who seem to hold the power, and the trust in one's own vision that is required:

I am conscious...of resisting the temptation to self-censor and write work which I 'think' will appeal to the mainstage companies. I continue to write what I want because I believe that I am still considered an emerging talent in the theatre industry and because I remain confident that my work, the work I want to write, will be performed in the near future.

I am mindful of the words of Jean Renoir, "In my view originality and success are strangers to one another; but I also hold that originality, despite appearances, will end by making itself felt, and easy success is soon forgotten."

Barbara Karpinski is a performance writer who radically challenges stereotypes. Her perception is that in theatre funding heads for what is safe.

I think socially acceptable middle class heterosexual feminism is very acceptable these days, but being a pan-sexual, bi-sexual lesbian, slut/writer/whore, my work is marginalised.

I don't identify and write from a female perspective — I am a gay man, a drag queen, a lesbian, a whore. I see my intensified sexuality as an advantage, but that's not peculiar to my gender. My basic aim is transgressive writing — beyond gender, beyond fear, and I hope one day I'll earn a decent living and become rich and famous.

Sue Anne Post:

I try to be a moving target. If you describe yourself as an ex-Mormon, feminist, lesbian, incest survivor, stand up comic, they get very perplexed.

The need to develop new form

Is it right to suggest that women's writing is different? Alison Lyssa wonders:

How does one get to be 'outside' or 'marginal'? Is it defined by the 'centre' i.e. by the person or organisation with the power to decide which work gets produced on a well-funded, well-publicised, well-lit stage? Does that person or body then impose upon the aspiring writers a set of rules and criteria that their work has to meet in order to be accepted? Defining 'mainstream' is difficult. It's a slippery concept, and a number of writers refuse to measure themselves against it.

Looking from another angle, does the woman writer who operates on what the mainstream perceives to be the 'fringe' actually see herself not as peripheral, but as seizing the day, defining herself and choosing to celebrate the way her work creates a new centre in a new space with an energy and a meaning that would be deflected, and perhaps destroyed, if that same work were to be performed on the conventional mainstage.

Writing from outside existing structures can provide women with opportunity to experiment and fly. Marion Campbell notes:

Perhaps a more iconoclastic approach to form is encouraged by women supporters of performance texts...

Performance writer-director-producer Jenny Kemp points to:

> *The need to develop new form ... new performance/performers' style ... as pre-existing structures do not necessarily suit.*

Jenny Kemp creates highly original work, which Peta Tait describes as:

> *...theatrical collages of visual imagery and soundscapes ... inviting the inner responses of the spectators ... a sanctuary for the spectator's inner world, inclusive of both its nightmarish and its harmonious dimensions.*[12]

Jenny Kemp herself says:

> *I can't find plays to satisfy me. I need to build my own. I form a theatrical world where we can experience everyday dream, myth and fantasy co-existing where linear time restraints are left behind. I just know I've got to build a different world...theatre reinforces the values of the mundane world through its form and content — it remakes the social world we live in. I find this problematic.*

Deborah Pollard writes:

> *More women now seem to dominate the 'fringe' not because they have been forced there, but because they relate better to the abstract forms, away from the male construct of the play.*

> *I have an outlook that has been created by the still tenuous position women have in the social and working world. My status as a woman (I believe) gives my work a critical edge.*

> *My work is written in poetry — I have found whilst the skill of the verse is acknowledged, set notions of character and dramatic action disallow people to think of it as a theatre piece...I'm not preoccupied with conventional definitions of character, action and drama, and so despite its force and fluidity, I found this (new work) a hard piece to sell. Elizabeth Jolley and Chris Wallace-Crabbe have commended this work, however I have not been able to find support for its performance.*

Did they imagine I didn't know what I was doing?

Noëlle Janaczewska is a writer moving between text and performance. She explains the deliberate process that goes into her experimental work.

> *Why did reviewers keep on telling me the 'rules' of theatre? Did they imagine I didn't know what I was doing, and if they 'put me right' I'd be OK!*

I'm interested above all in ideas; in abstractions and metaphors, in narrative explorations and the rhythms, materialities and idiosyncrasies of language, in a sense of character rather than realistic biographies. My work uses theatre and performance processes to investigate these ideas. I reject the head-heart opposition of intellect and emotion. For me, ideas can be passionate and the emotions are not without reason and circumspection. I like to think that my writing works with an associative, poetic kind of logic rather than with a dramatic logic of character journeys, plot development and conflict. In fact, I do not believe that conflict is necessary to make dynamic, enjoyable and challenging theatre, and I certainly do not believe in rules. Rules are not neutral and value-free, but serve particular interests and are answerable to specific histories.

Nor do I countenance the old cliché: "learn the rules first then you can break them". It seems to me the moment you posit rules you have created a centre and a periphery; a relationship of authority and opposition, a context in which any work perceived to be 'breaking the rules' can be safely shifted to the margin... It is therefore somewhat distressing when I see work reviewed in terms of 'the rules of theatre' — even when I've spelt out in program notes what I am and am not interested in exploring.

This has luckily not happened so much with recent work, but was a feature of two earlier scripts, Shoreline *and* The History of Water/Huyen Thoai Mot Giong Nuoc. *A number of reviews began with the re-iteration of these so-called 'rules of theatre'; chastised me for my lack of 'action' (another of those terms like 'conflict' and 'character journey' that I dislike for the ways they are used to censor and control) and overly abstract and intellectual themes.*

To begin with this made me feel like a disobedient schoolgirl, and then I wondered if those reviewing my work thought I was so stupid I wasn't aware of what I was doing and needed to be set back on the right track?

Fortunately I remembered something the French writer, film-maker and artist Jean Cocteau once said: "Take whatever it is that critics most despise about your work and cultivate it all you can, for that is the essence and distinctive strength of your work".

The 'soft' end

Many respondents see themselves as having an ambivalent relationship with the fields of community theatre and Theatre For Young People(TYP), also known as Theatre In Education (TIE) and youth theatre, where they are provided with commissioned, often regular, work. Many refer to work in this field with great pleasure and respect for the work, its audiences and the people who work there.

Experienced writers such has Anne Brookman have committed years of energy to work in young people's theatre.

Jenny Swain:

> *Half of my work is community based. It seems there are more women writing and directing in community theatre than men. There are a number of possible reasons for this. I believe that, although there are exceptions, women tend to have more developed skills that are conducive to this kind of work; listening skills, ability to empathise, nurturing - ability to validate other people's experiences, ability and willingness to adapt our writing skills to other people's needs.*

Yet writers also acknowledge that the income which this field pays them, and the status it attracts, indicate that the society we live in places a lesser value on it than it does on the work that appears on the mainstage before a subscription audience. Several award-winning writers whose work for community theatre is highly respected speculated that the very fact that they have written for community/youth theatre may mean that they are undervalued or ignored by mainstage directors.

Peta Murray's *Wallflowering* has been one of the most popular successes in Australian theatre since its premiere at the Canberra Theatre Company in 1989. Since then, however, Peta Murray's commissions have all been from TYP and community theatre. We might ask, why? *Wallflowering* was written on spec, not to a commission. Peta muses:

> *Sometimes wonder if I'm offered more work in TYP and community theatre because I'm a woman. The 'soft' end — certainly the lower paying end.*

Peta adds that 'soft' is not her own, but others' view.

Catherine Fargher writes:

> *My main professional work has been in the community theatre area and I have difficulty in accessing or being considered for writing in mainstream areas.*

Belinda Bradley explains there is still a struggle to make a living and to fight a feeling that her work is somehow marginalised:

> *Most of my work has been self-initiated. Even the puppet project, which Terrapin has now bought and will produce later this year, came about by my showing a rough draft of a script to the Artistic Director which she happened to like.*
>
> *I was interested to know that Terrapin approached some male writers for their upcoming (puppetry) project Desires, all of whom turned the work*

*down, and consequently there are five female playwrights involved, myself
included.*

*I have made very little money from playwriting to date and often wonder
why I persevere, but I do.*

*My work has been critically well received, in some cases very well
received, but there aren't enough adult theatres in this country, and
certainly not enough that are willing to take risks.*

Some worry about the effect of working in these areas on their future
professional development. Mardi McConnochie points out:

*Having done work in youth theatre and women's theatre may prove to be a
hindrance to me in the future (although I hope not). I am interested in
doing big mainstream plays on big stages in front of big audiences, and
there is a perception (especially in Sydney) that youth theatre and women's
theatre are ghettos where the untalented go to die.*

Janie Conway whose *Hitchoni* was group developed by Byron Bay Youth
Theatre, points out that in regional areas local newspapers and critics will accord
youth theatre the same respect and review space as adult professional theatre.
This is increasingly happening in major centres and reflects the quality of the
work.

Virginia Baxter acknowledges the innovations made in community theatre:

*Innovations in language and form that women have contributed to youth
and community theatre writing have never really been acknowledged for
their importance to the broader theatre community. Community and youth
theatres have been working for years with 'actual speech', but only when
Aftershocks written by Paul Brown with the Newcastle community became
a play in a city theatre did this form of writing receive acclaim and
publication follow. Similarly women have been using the ensemble form
for decades, but public acclaim goes to the ensemble work of John Bell,
Jim Sharman and Neil Armfield*

Peta Tait comments on Vitalstatistix, one of the most impressive community
theatre groups:

*Vitalstatistix might be categorised as creating community-based women's
theatre, especially since eleven out of fifteen productions have been
performed in their own local community at Port Adelaide...(However)
from the outset, Vitalstatistix have produced original full-length plays
written either by group members or other playwrights. These insightful
and humorous dramas show women characters trying to reconcile the
conflict between political idealism and the pragmatic circumstances of*

their lives in ways which fall outside the more straightforward feminist positions adopted in their issue-based productions ... These full-length plays also demonstrate the unique status of Vitalstatistix in Australian theatre in shaping new directions for women's theatre groups.[13]

Yes, but who wrote what?

Many writers suggested that women find particular strengths in working collaboratively, with male and female performers or writers or with other artists.

Margaret Fischer writes:

I believe that collaboration with other women is easier for me — I've collaborated with men in the past. Also I believe I have a unique perspective as a woman.

Dina Panozzo:

Just telling a story burning to be told to my collaborators was the beginning. I acted out my story-telling, we noted it down, called in others — choreographer, video-maker — to help me create structures and shapes for my story, my words. Improvisation and discussion and sometimes straight out writing on the page, all of this led me to find my 'original voice'. No one else's sound, just my own unique sound or sounds. The noise inside me became a legitimate driving force. The writer in me emerged.

Virginia Baxter has worked for a long time within a collaborative writing frame

In 1987 with Keith Gallasch I formed Open City a company producing collaborative performance works for theatre, galleries and radio and since 1994 a national performance publication, Real Time. *In each of Open City's productions, I have been co-writer and co-producer...The process of the writing is different in each case but all the works are developed in collaboration with a variety of other artists (visual artists, sound artists, composers, choreographers and other experts such as interior designers, air traffic controllers, interpreters, health workers, a ten year old girl). In each, I have written significant solo and dialogue pieces as well as co-writing with Keith and devising texts with other artists (always equally male and female). I sense sometimes that this means I'm not regarded as a 'proper' writer. People often want to know exactly who wrote what. And oddly, though Open City is a company that works very much with language, we often find ourselves included in the category of 'non-text based' performance. Though our works have always been critically praised for their innovation, no work has been published, save in journals.*

On the other hand as a woman working in this area I feel a distinct advantage. In our own and other performance companies, structures tend to be non-hierarchical, collaborative, offering the freedom to write. As someone who started out as an actor, I have had the space and time to become a writer and a producer of work and to encourage others to write.

When I started writing in 1983 with a 'solo' performance, many women were creating one-woman shows, i.e. writing collaboratively, co-devising, often beginning with a physical scenario and a text that developed through improvisation. These works made significant contributions to innovation in theatrical form. Similarly, the work in the early 1980's of women like Jan Cornall and Elizabeth Drake, Home Cooking Company and especially Gillian Jones' Anorexia Sometimes *(in 1982) were inspirations for me. But in the scheme of things these works didn't make it into the wider arena. They were discounted as simply polemical or personal (sometimes even 'therapeutic') having no significance beyond the original performance.*

More recently many women writers have been attracted by the freedoms offered in new performance forms. A short list of the many established and emerging writer-performers includes artists as diverse as Lyndal Jones, Barbara Campbell, Linda Sproul, Amanda Stewart, Ania Walwicz, Jai McEnery, Meme Thorne and Regina Heilmann, Club Swing, The Partyline, Noelle Janaczewska, Victoria Spence, Deborah Pollard, Anna Gibbs, Annette Tesoriero, Peggy Wallach, Crying in Public Places, Angharad Wynn-Jones, Monica Barone, Margaret Cameron, Kathleen Fallon, Dina Panozzo, Bronwyn Calcutt and Clare Grant. Because they don't conform to conventional structures, these writers challenge critics and audiences alike. Publication of their works is seen as difficult because they combine languages (words, visuals, music, dance, technology) and demand that non-verbal aspects of the performance be included. So although much of this work has its own growing audience and is acknowledged internationally, in Australia it's largely under-resourced. The areas of writing in which many women writers thrive are made less visible, less significant.

Mickey Furuya, who wrote a number of works in collaboration with the Sydney Front, including the award-winning *Woman in the Wall*, co-written with Clare Grant and others, points out that contradictions can emerge in the process of collaborative writing.

I was enrolled in an MA in Writing (since abandoned) while working with Sydney Front on First and Last Warning. *I found it unexpectedly difficult to resolve issues between myself as writer, as creator of the text, and the collaborative, deconstructing narrative developed by the group.*

All this in a performance situated in a broader examination of dominance, hierarchies and difference, confronting the spectator as feminine, while disturbing the boundary between spectator and performer. In the end I discovered that my work on this text would be disallowed for my thesis, as the text was collaborative, and having already been performed, was considered a 'published', i.e. ineligible, work.

Barbara Bossert-Ramsay points to one of the problems of partnerships:

For some years I wrote with a male partner. It was always assumed, erroneously, that he wrote and I sort of 'helped' or 'edited' or was some kind of 'Girl Friday'.

Not taken seriously as a genre

Some women writers have moved to newer fields such as music theatre. Jennie Swain comments:

My experience as a songwriter/comedian/cabaret artist/composer and deviser is relevant to my writing work for theatre. Most of this experience seems to be undervalued and my desire to create musical comedy that is socially relevant leads me to an undefined area; musical comedy is not taken seriously as a genre. There have been some major flops in Australia because producers are under the misguided notion that audiences must have spectacle with their shows.

I believe there are many skilled writers and performers working in the cabaret area who have developed a keen understanding of how to communicate with an audience and how to convey complex ideas without boring or alienating them. These are the artists that should be nurtured into writing music theatre; these are people with something to say.

Hilary Bell is another writer with a strong commitment to developing musical theatre. She has discussed the fact that the form itself dictates a need for compromise, because of the necessity for collaboration between writer and composer. She rejoices in her capacity to collaborate with Stephen Rae:

You don't want to be too like-minded, because part of the joy of collaborating is springing off each other's ideas, coming in with things the other would never have thought of...There's something very creative about compromise.

In looking at the career paths of many of our respondents, it is possible to see that women do combine creativity with flexibility, both in collaborative writing relationships and in determining the most appropriate form or genre for a piece. Stella Kent has developed a play and then decided that it worked more effectively on radio. Sonia Ryan has written plays but her most recent work is a semi-operatic collaboration with singer Annette Tesoriero.

Teresa Crea is one respondent who combines an extraordinary number of roles:

My role as a writer has intrinsically been interwoven with my other 'roles' as director, devisor, dramaturg and even translator. Occasionally this has been because I have wanted it so, but for the most part it has been by default. We just do not have a pool of bilingual writers, dramaturgs etc. that can truly represent the cultural diversity of this country. What's more, everything from our training institutions to channels of promotion and distribution still operate almost exclusively within mono-cultural frameworks.

Less to do with gender

There are some factors in the theatre industry that women report as obstacles, but recognise as less to do with gender than other issues. These therefore affect male writers as well. Together these factors form a picture of a theatre industry that is perceived to be less encouraging to writers than desirable. Reading the responses to the survey one gets a sense that writers perceive they have a threefold struggle: to have their work and their skills taken seriously; to have their work comprehended and developed with sensitivity; and to have it produced free of distortions.

At very basis is the need to establish a canon of Australian writing for theatre. Mardi McConnochie points to:

...the importance of setting up an Australian canon of work, so that new plays don't just get performed once and then disappear into the ether.

Some problems in developing this Australian canon have to do with the establishment of an acceptable development route. Margaret Kirby writes:

This is a very cruel and hard industry...it is uninterested in new playwrights, will support the development of text but has very little intention of ever mounting anything. In Melbourne with the loss of The Church and Theatreworks there is no middle career theatre space between La Mama and Playbox where exciting, brave, large scale new work can be mounted, with the exception of Courthouse (which is small and "dreadful") and Napier Street which is fearsomely in demand.

I hope my next play has a somewhat smoother ride

Some women feel they are struggling against attitudes which reduce their skills and deny them maturity and feel they are trapped in a development ghetto.

Sarah Brill reports:

> *...there seem to be more women participating in development programs, proportionally to production.*

Sally Richardson is puzzled by:

> *Interest in funding my development as an emerging artist (not in the actual work itself!)*

Monica Raszewski has also encountered hurdles to actually having her work performed:

> *I started writing for performance in 1985. I co-wrote a play with three other women writers and it was performed at La Mama. After the experience of a group devised project I decided to write a play exploring some of my ideas in greater depth and on my own. I wrote* Change of Heart *which was workshopped by Playworks in 1988. The play had a public reading at Belvoir Street Theatre and as a result of this reading it was picked up by the ANPC and was read again at the 1989 Sydney Carnivale.*

> *The play seemed to generate quite a bit of interest but was never produced. In 1990 I became more interested in fiction writing and until recently this has been my primary focus.*

> *However, in 1993 I looked at* Change of Heart *again and renamed it* Suitcases. *I worked on the script again because I believed it still had something worthwhile which could be developed. After a major rewrite I sent the play to TheatreWorks in Melbourne. The play was well received and there was a strong possibility that it would be produced in 1994. Unfortunately TheatreWorks lost most of their funding that year. I then sent the play to Playbox. Aubrey Mellor encouraged me to make a few changes and send it in again. The play was selected for another public reading this time as part of Playbox's* Theatre in the Raw *series. After this reading I met with Kim Durban from Playbox who gave a written report which was most useful.* Suitcases *is now a completely different play called* Forest *and Chris Williams from the ABC would like to produce it for radio in the near future. I hope my next play has a somewhat smoother ride.*

I find the attitude of theatre companies to writers wearing

Debra Oswald outlines the struggle experienced by many writers in getting their scripts beyond a development stage into production by a theatre company.

> *In general I feel that the problems of being a playwright in Australia now are less to do with gender than other issues. The fact is that there are a*

very small number of berths for a new Australian play in any year,
whether by a man or a woman. A small number of writers consistently fills
those slots and I suppose men dominate that established group. I find the
attitude of theatre companies to writers wearing. Writers are supposed to
be grateful supplicants in the process. The fact that a reasonably
experienced writer like me finds it almost impossible to get a reading at
all is bewildering and distressing.

Oswald has a strong awareness of the non-professional treatment she believes she has experienced.

Responses were often very very slow in coming, only after much hassling
by my agent. It seems difficult to get scripts read by artistic directors. Play
readers are often in the position of powerful gatekeepers and the
playreaders/dramaturgs themselves are not accountable and not always
any good.

Some theatre companies and individual directors have never responded. Queensland Theatre Company, for example, took almost three years.

The fact that this play (Gary's House) *was not considered worthy of even*
preliminary attention (despite my reasonable track record) is one reason
why I will not write for the theatre again in the foreseeable future.

Dags was an AWGIE award-winning comedy about adolescence yet still had no easy run as a production.

After Toe Truck and Q Theatre productions, no theatre companies wanted
to pick up the play. As a result, two actors from the show formed their own
company and mounted two very successful national tours. Since then,
various regional companies, amateur groups and schools have done
productions. No 'mainstream' company has ever shown any interest.

Another writer to comment critically on the poor response from companies to work submitted is successful dramatist Joanna Murray-Smith.

Love Child *and* Honour *have been and are in the process of being sent to*
lots of different theatre companies in Australia and overseas. Playbox
handles most of this on my behalf.

Certainly, the English theatres (about six in London: the Bush, the
Almeida, the Royal Court and others) sent back reports from artistic
directors which is more than you can say about Australian theatre
administrations in the most part, from my experience.

Many other writers mention the slowness and inefficiency of theatre companies in responding to work submitted or indeed providing to writers, after successful productions, promised packages of photographs and reviews.

Dramaturgy is often the first thing to be cut

Other general problems that respondents report include: "a lack of good dramaturgy in theatres" and a tendency for funding to go to "commercial run-of-the-mill work".

Mardi McConnochie makes a strong case for the importance of improved dramaturgy in Australia.

> *Unfortunately, dramaturgy is often the first thing to be cut when budgets are tight, or it's a job given to people who really want to be directors or writers or who don't really know how to be dramaturgs. I've had sessions with dramaturgs who were supposed to be helping me improve my plays where I spent the whole time explaining the play to them. It seems to me that it is vitally important that we develop a critical culture around theatre (in dramaturgy, in theatre reviewing, everywhere). It is also important that women be a vocal and prominent part of that culture.*

One playwright commented that the company which had commissioned her cancelled their planned production of her play:

> *...the Artistic Director was overbearing and patronising. He dismissed the play at first draft and refused to consult the local Aboriginal community on the play.*

The playwright warns others to be protective of their work:

> *Be sure that your play is ready before presenting it to artistic directors, particularly if your first instinct is that this person doesn't trust you. If it's possible for you to develop the play with someone else, such as Playworks, or ANPC, do that, or ask for a dramaturg to be included in the commission, and make sure your dramaturg is not the artistic director.*

Virginia Jane Rose notes:

> *The main problems seem to face all writers for performance: being excluded from the bulk of production development; trying to work with colleagues (not writers, other roles) who don't try to comprehend the complexity of the writing process, the layers of meaning in the whole.*

Therese Radic:

> *I don't know why directors assume that they know best. The first production is a crucial reading.*

I'll write where I'm wanted

A number of respondents who have written award-winning work are being lost to the stage in the short term, or even indefinitely, because they are finding it a great deal easier to earn their living writing for television or film where they are welcomed rather than being supplicants as they feel in theatre. One writer said that to write for the stage could mean writing on spec for a year with no income, whereas television offered regular commissions. Debra Oswald, Katherine Thomson, Tobsha Learner, Linda Aronson, Jan Cornall, Suzanne Hawley and Hannie Rayson all write regularly for the screen.

Writing for television and film may be a sensible professional development for many writers. They have a chance to earn reasonable money and to gain larger audiences and possibly international recognition. For many women writers these areas draw on the collaborative and imaginative skills they have developed in their writing for theatre.

Debra Oswald explains:

> *Given that in the fields of TV, children's literature etc., good writers are wooed, there is little incentive to beat my head against the doors of the major theatre companies. I will write where I'm wanted and not for the theatre, where I am made to feel like a nuisance and a desperate.*

Patricia Johnson does not see herself as facing specific obstacles compared with men, but finds writing for theatre is 'hard and getting harder — for everybody':

> *However I have found that a big success — in theatre, TV and film — didn't necessarily lead onward and upward, whereas it (seems to) for the directors involved.*

Oh God not the writer again!

It seems from the comments of a number of respondents that it is hard to create a sense of worth from within — particularly in a society which prevailingly equates value with dollars and simultaneously finds ways of paying less to women for the work they do.

Many writers also point to their perception that in Australia writers for performance, and in particular for the traditional theatre, are more neglected as partners and collaborators than they are in other theatre traditions. In addition, they may have particularly difficult relationships with directors.

Jill Shearer writes of her good experience with plays produced in New York and in the West End:

> *In New York there is a long time tradition of working with the writer, and I*

felt a complete acceptance which was fruitful for the production of the play. It showed that writers could be usefully and excitingly brought in as part of the team.

One writer comments that "they behave as if they're doing you a favour".

Jan Cornall:

Invisibility is a reality for both women and writers. I write to become visible, to be heard in the larger community. Sometimes when your work is performed you in fact feel more invisible than ever.

I think as women writers we must continue to push the boundaries of theatre, to be seen and heard in the way we want, in the way that suits us. Only then can we hope to become truly visible both to ourselves and our audience/community.

Alma de Groen writes:

I've never enjoyed looking back , and when I tried to in this case (and I did try many times!) much of my theatre history seemed like a form of aversion therapy. The only way to keep writing is not to look back otherwise I'd stop dead in my tracks. There were some wonderful experiences with extraordinary people, but too much of the time I was the bad fairy at the christening ("Oh, God, not the writer again!").

In the firing line

Dorothy Hewett sees theatre as a contentious medium.

I think the very fact of writing in such a public forum puts you in the firing line, much more so than if you went off and wrote a novel quietly in the back room somewhere and then people read it. It's not that same sort of confrontational situation as the theatre ... I think the theatre as a form invites confrontation for everyone.

Another view comes from Linda Aronson, who has been writing professionally for performance for 18 years.

Theatre is a collaborative medium and it is unrealistic to expect to sail through without conflict somewhere along the way. I have had many very positive experiences with dramaturgs, directors and actors of both sexes. I don't feel the conflicts I've had have been gender specific. I do feel that writers as a group lack negotiation skills in conflict situations. We are not good at staying calm while asserting authority and brokering solutions favourable to ourselves. And when we lose our tempers we lose our power. Assertiveness Training workshops might be a practical way to help us maximise our power in the workplace.

He succeeded in totally reversing the meaning of the play

The fear of distortion of their text affects all writers. Nonetheless some respondents reported particular problems when a script was deliberately misunderstood or misinterpreted. It is possible that these difficulties, which face all writers, male and female and particularly those at the beginning of their career, are exacerbated when the director is male and the writer female.

Some experienced determined efforts by directors and/or actors to change the writer's text and its presentation. Respondents saw this as an attempt to distort the meaning of their work so that the challenge it potentially represented to the world view of the director and/or actors was reduced, deflected or removed altogether. Another form of censorship is reported by women writers whose characters are found to be unacceptable by male or female actors. Stories of walkouts, misrepresentations in performance and characters having words put in their mouths by actors and directors seeking to make characters more 'believable' are not uncommon.

Margaret Kirby writes:

A director identified totally with the central male character (an emotionally destitute middle-aged man, but well-rounded and written with empathy). In production he succeeded in totally reversing the meaning of the play:(from this) — unless men grow emotionally the important women in their lives will try to help them for so long before they leave them; (to this) — the men in the play are complete victims of irrational, vindictive women.

He did this despite the fact that it made no sense. He even went so far as to add and remove lines ... It had never occurred to me that someone could take something written over two years with great love and attention to detail and reverse it like that. By the end of the second scene he had disempowered every female character. I was chastised for my strong emotional reaction to his work and reminded that writers never see their work performed exactly how they imagine it.

If readers of the text have no feminist understanding, or, worse, if they have a reason to protect the dominant paradigm ... they will not be reading positive meaning into a strong female character, and they will valorise a male's weaknesses and hypocrisy because they empathise.

Elizabeth Spencer gives us an example of a male dramaturg who tried to pressure her to censor her own work (for her own good!):

...he complained about my portrayal of the male character ... claiming he was a stereotype and I would get into trouble with the critics if I kept the character as written. I felt this was unfair, as I'd only portrayed my experience of a particular person I know, without intending to make any comment on his moral character whatsoever. Perhaps there is a fair amount of insecurity out there still.

Another writer reports:

...severe problems last year, mainly caused by a lack of proper leadership checking the extremely aggressive behaviour of my director who had prior announced "I don't believe in what this play says". As a writer who's been told I fit in well with most actors and directors, I have been practically banned from rehearsals. At what appeared to be nevertheless a successful opening night, when I mentioned a couple of changes to an actress, she said "What really worries me is the director's projected meeting tomorrow afternoon with a view to deleting all of P's dialogue from the last scene". I gave up then. The AWG solicitor took over.

Anna North recalls an occasion when:

I had a male director tell a group of actors that I "didn't know what I was talking about". Given that it was my play and my workshop, I thought this was inappropriate, unhelpful and very rude. I don't think he would have said this to or about a male colleague. Certainly not in his presence.

These problems do not only occur with male directors and actors, but also with women. Lois Achimovich reports:

I disagreed with a female director about the portrayal of an 'abandoned wife' character and with a male about a violent man, whose violence I believe was diluted by the direction. I lost both struggles.

Paula Abood emphasises that difficulties are exacerbated with work which challenges other prejudices.

*Promoting culturally diverse works while maintaining the integrity of the work (*Politics of belly dancing*) is/was fraught with difficulty. Undoing stereotypes and expectations of 'other' cultures is part of the process; essential in terms of providing a context/some understanding of different 'forms' and issues affecting/ confronting Arab-Australian women.*

The male playwrights I know appear to be more confident

Large numbers of respondents from emerging to experienced writers report on problems to do with self-esteem which affects their ability to fight for the integrity of their work or to establish themselves as professionals.

A successful playwright observes:

> *(There is) a sense of affirmative action in place in that companies do seem to actively seek women's work. I would temper this, however, with the observation that women don't seem to expect to work full-time, or earn a living, from the theatre when compared to male playwrights.*

A number of respondents comment on the internalisation of this lack of confidence in one's ability and the struggle to maintain self-esteem when one sees one's own and other women's work frequently undervalued.

Jo Fleming:

> *This is very difficult to quantify. I believe that my gender has impeded my career in theatre. In part there are fewer opportunities and, in part, it is self-perpetuated. I simply do not have the self-confidence of many of my male colleagues.*

Suzanne Spunner:

> *I took a long time to acknowledge/claim my desire/right to be an artist/ assert creative ego; but it may have as much to do with class as well as gender. The lack of self-esteem may reflect and then unwittingly reinforce the view of the market that women's work has a lesser value.*

Patricia Cornelius comments:

> *I think that, along with most women writers for performance, my work has been largely overlooked. This is because our work is considered less, and because we are poor sellers of our work and ourselves.*

Mary Hutchison:

> *It's hard to know whether these (obstacles) are not also to do with lack of formal qualifications, lack of performance and directorial skills, age, personality, but I feel it's harder to assert my ideas as 'real' ideas — and to achieve credibility.*
>
> *In working with men I have sometimes felt like a secretary rather than a writer.*

Another observes:

> *The obstacles I face are all of my own making, and to do with confidence, with claiming a place, with productivity (which is either due to faith in one's imagination or a belief that whatever you have to say will be important enough for a play). The male playwrights that I know appear to*

be more confident, and claim other roles in the theatre such as dramaturg or director when not writing.

Jodi Gallagher:

Both times that I've had work accepted at Playbox I've been given a bit of a talking to about the fact that I don't routinely submit my work — and from now on I probably will. There seems to be a perception there that female playwrights don't follow through professionally by submitting their work to mainstream companies, that we feel somehow intimidated by the structure ... Personally, I think that it's more general than this, it's not just women playwrights who don't feel that they'll find a sympathetic reception at mainstream level — it's a general feeling on the fringe. But again, it's probably exacerbated by being a woman. So all the difficulties experienced by a playwright working on the fringe and trying to break into the mainstream are made just that little bit more problematic by female gender. Yet the awareness of the problem, of the need for more equitable programming is an advantage.

Linden Wilkinson:

I had low expectations initially; this was a great advantage, because creating was relatively stress-free. Having low expectations meant that I didn't have a desire to strive for clarity, for wholeness in my work ... if I did some parts well, that was good enough. So I feel I've wasted time by not taking things very seriously. I also thought that I didn't have anything important to say. My areas of interest are the world within and the immediate world without. I didn't see for a very long time, that because everybody else's characters talked about politics and genocide that they too were simply expressing the same areas of interest in a different way.

Peta Murray also wonders:

...if men doing similar work face the same self-made obstacles re self-esteem, the value of one's work, one's right to be doing it.

Damage Control

There are suggestions from some writers that women may be particularly sensitive and may take some time to recover from damning criticism or poor reviews.

Catherine Fargher points to the damage that occurred when her work was attacked years ago, and her determination now to keep writing:

My first foray into writing was in (gasp) the Adelaide Law School Review.

All my scripts went in front of a group (let's say Cabal) of Catholic Law Students — all boys and wanna-be Monty Pythons. They rejected all my scripts on current affairs — never a hint of trying them out or developing them. I was able to perform one script of my own, a parody on Margaret Thatcher's speeches for invading the Falklands. Apart from that I was relegated to being the lead female role — Annie T. Ugly in They root horses, don't they. *You have to laugh. It's a long time ago but I see it as a telling example. A lot of those boys did go on to produce, write or act in TV comedy, an area which I had been very interested in. I think that affirmative action at that level, or if I had been more of a feminist at the time, would have made a difference — although I probably would never have done the* Law School Review *to start with!*

But as a young woman writer ... I lost a lot of confidence and assumed that my work was not good. There was no positive feedback about the script I did develop (except from people in the audiences). I think at a young age many women lack the sort of conviction/bravado that boys have. I'm pleased to report that I am developing it now, 15 years later!

It is not just young writers who react badly to these setbacks. Therese Radic is one of Australia's longest-standing playwrights and has had a number of successful plays produced both in Australia and internationally over the last twenty years. One problem she identifies is:

Lack of women directors who understand my point of view makes it difficult for me to be adequately produced. Male directors seem to find it necessary to impose their egos on the play in order to stamp it as theirs.

She expresses particular concern about Barrie Kosky's 1992 production of her play *The Emperor Regrets* which she found "deeply offensive...I have not written a play since".

I felt isolated and unappreciated until I found Playworks

Writing for the theatre is a craft that requires an apprenticeship. To read the responses to our survey is to become aware of how long and difficult that apprenticeship can be. Many respondents commented that they would have given up many times if it had not been for the on-going support of particular individuals or groups who had nurtured them, including particular theatre companies, and organisations such as Playworks.

We hope our survey reached Julie Janson in a passing moment of gloom, for she writes that the experience of a woman writing for performance is one of "unrelenting misery":

I felt very isolated and unappreciated until I found Playworks.

Janie Conway points to the advantage of "a supportive network of women's organisations" which she experienced when she was a member of the Pram Factory/Women's Performing Group. At the same time she lists as an obstacle for women the lack of acceptance "in the broader sphere outside of a women's network".

Catherine Fargher comments:

> *Most theatre networks in NSW, apart from community theatre, seem to be set up to advantage men. It's hard to be more specific. It means you have to network at levels which not all women feel they can access. Only when there are specific networks set up by/for women is there an advantage (for women writers for performance.)*

Patricia Johnson points to a different aspect of the problem of access to networks:

> *I am not interested in just ultra-specific areas — i.e. 'women's' theatre — as a writer. Therefore, so-called 'networking' in decision-making circles I have found difficult.*

Patricia Jones:

> *I mistakenly relied on men for criticism. I am isolated in as far as connections. I have corrected this by joining a women's group. I trust women more.*

Sometimes Playworks has a problem in the perception that it is Sydney-based and not easily accessible. Therese Radic explains her sense of distance:

> *Unfortunately I live in Melbourne and Playworks people don't know me and it's expensive to go to Sydney for a period. Otherwise I would long ago have sought Playworks help over several projects. I feel there is some sort of a barrier between me and this group. Is it my age? What?*

Playworks has also been concerned to note that a couple of writers from other states did not know of our existence.

> *PS. It's very comforting to know/find out that an organisation like Playworks exists. Can I please become a member?*

Playworks will continue to increase its activity as a national organisation cheered by the praise received from a number of respondents for the encouragement, network and support it provides.

Belinda Bradley:

> *The only benefit I have experienced being a woman playwright is through Playworks, because they are an organisation that works with women only.*

Sonia Ryan is also encouraging:

Playworks have supported me and my writing; have given me encouragement; have put me in contact with performers who have become my friends and supporters and with whom I continue to work.

Funding bodies are currently women-oriented and although I've had no personal experience of that orientation, Playworks have which is specially advantageous to me as it is to all women writers.

I literally wouldn't be doing it without their support

An interesting fact to emerge from the survey was that a number of agents approached for lists of women writers were not immediately aware of the number of women writers for performance on their books. Some expressed alarm at the small number. A surprising finding was how few women writers have agents - even those with many critical successes and many years experience.

The low representation by agents underlines the importance of support networks and also of sponsors and mentors as sources of support and advice. A number of writers acknowledge how important specific mentors have been in the development of their craft and their careers. In particular women directors and administrators have played a very important role. Jodi Gallagher indicates that:

La Mama has been the main support for my writing — I literally wouldn't be doing it without their support, and specifically the support of Liz Jones who has not only produced my work but has been there for me in more ways than I could count. La Mama does seem to be particularly sympathetic to the work of women writers.

Anna Broinowski:

Mainstream theatrical networks are still run by men; but I feel that a nurturing and supportive female network is also emerging now.

Marion Campbell was approached by Noelle Janaczewska as director to adapt a novel into a performance text. Similarly Sue Woolf began writing for theatre when Lynette Curran asked her to adapt her novel *The Painted Woman* for a women directors' season at Sydney's Belvoir Street Theatre.

Ruth Conley Watson points to the special advantage of:

Women (both performers and writers) who encourage me and feed my inspiration.

Mardi McConnochie argues for the importance of women directors.

Women writers need more women directors, for a number of reasons. It seems to me that plays get onto the stage because one person (a director, the director of a company, a producer) believes passionately in the play (or sometimes the writer) and is willing to walk through fire to get it on the stage. It is often the case that a woman director will share with a woman writer a particular sensibility, a set of experiences, stylistic or thematic concerns, or an interest in a particular story. This is not to say that all plays by women should be directed by women, or that plays by men should be directed by men. The last thing we need is an official gender apartheid.

A play directed by someone who fully understands it is more likely to be successful, and a fully-rounded, fully-satisfying production of a play written by a woman can only be good for business. The more successful women playwrights there are the harder it becomes to dismiss our work as ghetto theatre for a minority. How 52% of the population became a minority is not entirely clear, but that remains the perception.

Several respondents pointed out how important it was that they had the support and encouragement of other women. A similar number of respondents reported that they had received encouragement and support from both women and men. One writer observed that men often have the support of women, professionally and personally, but the reverse is not so often the case.

Beatrix Christian has enjoyed the support of male mentors but sees advantages and disadvantages in this.

It is contradictory — I've had a lot of mentoring and support from older men in the industry — I suspect it's easier for them to patronise you as a woman coming up, and I mean that in the positive sense — but it's always more of a disadvantage as a woman. Mentoring is generally done by men because there aren't many women in the industry to do it. In the beginning I had support from Ken Healey at NIDA and Michael Gow at STC — they're prepared to help you with your work to a certain point, but that doesn't mean that they'll trust the work ultimately.

What is clear is that it may be a matter of luck or good fortune for writers to be given the personal and professional support that enables their writing to thrive.

All things to all women

Writers must at times struggle against criticism and lack of support from other women.
Hannie Rayson writes:

Interestingly, I feel I've suffered at the hands of female critics. Certainly I have had bad reviews from men. But there is a tone of vitriol in three particular instances which has struck me as being different from exercising a critical voice. It is not the substance of the reviews, but the tone which concerns me — vituperative, angry. Why is this?

Linda Aronson:

There is sometimes a tendency in audiences to expect women writers to be all things to all women. This is an understandable response, but it can put us under great pressure.

An additional effect of the high expectations placed on women writers by other women is that there may be a tendency to present all women characters as ideals, to self-censor criticism. Writers at a recent Women's Screen Writing Conference also spoke about self-censorship among women writers. Hannie Rayson reports:

...while we don't all share the same 'prohibited zones' we do all feel the need to contextualize them. So in portraying a stupid woman for example one feels compelled to throw in a casual aside (a few scenes later) that she actually suffered a head injury from a road accident.

Dorothy Hewett argues against this:

I wanted to try and create a range of woman characters who had something to say about the condition of women, whether positive or negative. I would hope that up to a point I succeeded in doing that. Certainly changing the balance for a while, anyway. I didn't just want to have positive characters all the time. Quite a lot of the characters in my plays are anything but leaders of the feminist movement — the very reverse, I think.

Fringes, margins and deserts

A number of respondents pointed out that the main problems faced by women writers in getting their work accepted by established producers apply to all writers who come in from the cold, the 'fringe', the margin, the desert, the western suburbs, or Western Australian, whether female, male, Aboriginal, multi-lingual, of culturally diverse background, or any other outsider to the power perceived to be held in the large subsidised theatres of eastern Australia. Marlish Glorie comments on the lack of opportunities in WA:

I tend to send my work over East — and in future will be sending it to England and Ireland.

Living in WA may, Heather Nimmo suggests, create more obstacles "to being considered an Australian playwright". This tendency to be denied recognition may be compounded "because I have written also for children and community theatre".

Another Western Australian Lois Achimovich also stresses the problem of distance, especially in Western Australia, and lack of contact with other writers, dramaturgs and theatre people, and the lack of female mentors:

> *Fortunately, Pippa Williamson has supported my writing. Without her, I would have given up.*

The things I've done to make a bob

Heather Nimmo pinned a note to her CV:

> *It shows you all the places I've lived (largely following my husband and his work opportunities) and the things I've done to make a bob, but wherever I've been and whatever I've else been doing, I've been writing and going to the theatre and supporting the arts in my community — however small. It's not just about plays written and performed (although that's important too). It's about what you've given and what you've received.*

Heather's CV shows a range of occupations from 1973 through to 1990: work in community welfare and psychology; remedial and mature-age teaching in English; tertiary teaching in Statistics and Behavioural Science; field-work in geology; historical research for mining companies and a five year stint as a self-employed tin miner.

Then a new heading 'Employment as Playwright/Scriptwriter' appears. Although her paid writing career began in 1986 with the writing of advertising copy, since 1990 all her employment listed is in connection with writing — from playwright-in residence to dramaturg, script-editor and tertiary teacher of writing for theatre and radio, from commissions and increasing royalties. Heather also has an active connection with community arts, as participant and instigator, sometimes in remote and country areas where she has lived, sometimes by connecting with far-flung community theatre groups who have heard about her plays and want to put one on. A few samples of her community work:

> 1987-88: Organised inaugural Poetry in the Pub readings at the historic Boulder Block Tavern.
>
> 1987: Wrote community musical *A Touch of Midas* for Kalgoorlie/Boulder
>
> 1988: Wrote *Ten Bog Brothers* for Kalgoorlie scouts and cubs to perform at bicentennial touring show.
>
> 1990: Wrote *Boots* for Junction Theatre Company to perform in workplaces.

A play about the empowerment of women. Research included interviewing women in blue collar jobs.

1994: Spoke to the Ladies Auxiliary of the AusIMM about mining and writing drama.

Heather Nimmo has brought experiences of theatre or other writing to a large number of people; *One Small Step* a one-woman play which toured widely and won a Western Australian Premiers Award in 1993, was seen by audiences of over 15,000.Her work history demonstrates the flexibility and self-motivation required by a woman writer moving constantly because of family responsibilities.

Who's looking after your kids?

Finally, a number of respondents comment on how their years of writing for theatre have been interrupted by the need to earn a larger income than they can as a writer. Nearly all the writers who list financial concerns as an obstacle to their writing add that they have children to support as well as themselves.

The demands of home and family are pressing for writers at particular points in their life cycle. The difficulties go beyond those related to finding child care. The years that women spend caring for home and family often produce a major hiatus in their writing careers and place them in difficulty with maintaining contacts and networks.

Elizabeth Spencer points to:

> *...the difficulty of finding time to do the work with a small child, the running of a household and the earning of a living.*

Child-care has certainly taken time for Jennifer Bethel. Her first play was written 1986/87; her second 1994/95, and none in between.

> *I was a single mother unable to afford to write during the day (i.e. full-time work) and unable to 'network' much on evenings and weekends because of that responsibility.*

Helen Bulley feels she has faced obstacles compared to men:

> *...but only because I've chosen to be with my three children — time is a precious commodity to writers who are mothers.*
>
> *I think it's probably my own rather reclusive nature that's kept me writing for radio instead of pursuing theatre — time too, and family, which is why women have always written novels and poetry rather than plays — You can do it at home, and you don't have to be involved in the teamwork situation of theatre.*

Tes Lyssiotis has found that being a mother (and all that entails) and a writer a problem. "Difficult - yet also an inspiration".

Marlish Glorie explains that:

Family commitments — and financial — have stalled my writing career. I think many women artists are in a similar position ...Late starters in writing because they are the main child carers, house-looker afters, as well as working for money. It leaves very little time for writing.

By the time one gets back to serious writing one's confidence has taken quite a battering — after years and years in domesticity. Basically the opportunities I do have to write result in rushed work. However despite all this, the latest two plays I have been working on, Midnight Matchmakers *and* The Garden, *have met with favourable comments.*

On the positive side — I see my future in writing plays...The lifetime I have spent being involved in other activities gives me, I feel, a wealth of life experience to draw from...

Virginia Jane Rose comments:

In early years of writing for performance I was a sole parent, so parental duties and pleasures naturally commanded time and energy. An on-going obstacle is the continuing (though challenged) dominance of men in theatre — specially in the 'epic' and 'big issue' areas I work in.

Fiona Navilly:

As a woman and mother of young children there is much I have not written or actively sought out because of my commitment to their needs. I call them silences (what has not been written) and also frustrations! Ever present consciousness of childcare needs and limits infringes on time spent in performers in the studio which is vital to my process.

Debra Hely:

The most difficult question wasn't asked. Time to write when working full time is the major hurdle — particularly large blocks of time to allow focus. Although some of [my] plays look like I've taken years and years to write, it's really a result of working on them during holidays; not very satisfactory at all.

Heather Nimmo sums up practical difficulties she has experienced:

Attending rehearsals at night, weekends. Networking.

Linda Aronson describes some difficulties:

When my kids were babies I was working as a scriptwriter, bearing a full workload even though I only had three days a week when I could work nine to five. It was impossible to work on plays at night — as one would normally do. I tried and made myself ill. Fortunately a grant from the Australia Council enabled me to keep going.

Sue Ingleton sums it all up:

Being a writer/performer means you get — all the glory, all the pain.

Being a female writer/performer means you get — Whose lookin' after your kids?

Being a female writer/performer in Australia means you get mostly reviewed by men who are jealous of all the glory, enjoy seeing you in pain and never, ever look after your kids.

In summary

Women writers welcome a sense of opportunities. More established writers feel that they have benefited, been sought out by companies. Emerging writers sense that there are real possibilities for them. There is a feeling of excitement among many respondents who see themselves as having a unique perspective and the skills to present it. They rejoice in favourable responses from their audience and from theatre critics.

Some issues raised by women writers are particularly relevant to all writers. They emphasise the importance of writers being valued by directors and theatre managements and performers as a crucial part of the collaborative team. Writers urge companies to respond quickly to their submission of scripts. They ask for improvements in dramaturgical support. They want be part of decisions about adjustments to plot-lines and characters.

Women speak of development, networking and collaboration as vital to their lives as writers. They value groups such as Playworks which put them in touch with other writers and directors. The female writer is offered far fewer mentors and role models than the male writer whose work has been more often performed and studied.

Some women speak of a fragile sense of self-esteem and setbacks that stop them writing for many years. Networks are important to build up the isolated writer and ensure that she values her own work and her views on how it may be produced.

Women draw confidence from the fact that well over half of the audience is female. Encouraged by the positive changes that have taken place and whatever the obstacles, most of the women responding show a determination to continue to express their point of view and to do it through their writing.

t h r e e

assisting women writers for performance

Many women writers who responded to our survey expressed the view that they have benefited from positive policies from funding bodies towards assistance to women's work. This is perceived as a marked change over the past ten years.

We have already discussed in Section 1 how the Australia Council introduced a policy of affirmative action in 1984, in response to research demonstrating the inequities experienced by women in access to grants. In that section we outlined the measures developed by the Council so that women could achieve a comparable standing to that of men.

The research demonstrated that less women applied for grants across all art-form boards, totalling 33% of all applications in 1982-3. Figures collected by the Australia Council on an annual basis since that time, and provided by their Strategy and Communications Branch, show a steady increase in the proportion of applications from individual women artists in all fields. In 1993-4, applications from women reached 46% of all applications, with 1,283 individual women applying for grants.

The Australia Council has also been active in ensuring that women apply for a level of funding equivalent to men. The 1983 research showed that not only did fewer women apply for grants, they applied in every art-form for lesser amounts. Women were more likely to apply, for example, for a Category B Fellowship than a category A. The gap has steadily been closing. By 1993-4, the average amount requested by females was almost equal to that requested by males - $19,922 by females and $20,582 by males. Interestingly, however, figures collected that year on applications for Australian Artists Creative Fellowships, the so-called 'Keatings' awarded to senior artists for long projects, showed that far fewer women had applied than men.

Over the ten years between 1983-4 and 1993-4, the proportion of total grants awarded to women increased from 41% to 48%. Similarly, the average grants to female and male artists have moved closer together. In 1988-89, the average grant to females slightly exceeded that for males. This was also the case in 1993-4, with female artists receiving an average grant of $13,722, and males $13,221. Thus the development of an awareness of patterns of discrimination has assisted individual women artists.

It was particularly interesting to Playworks to see what had happened in the specific area of writing for performance. We found that the Australia Council does direct high numbers of grants to women's work, affirming the perception of many of our respondents that it offered a strong example of positive affirmation of women's capabilities and provided increased opportunities for women. Overall in the Literature Board, the success rate for women receiving grants has risen over the ten years from 33% to almost 50%.

It is extremely important for writers to be funded. Funding provides particular benefits: time to write, an opportunity to develop craft and skills, opportunity for travel for experience and research, time out from other employment and, if the project is a commission, the chance of seeing work performed.

The Australia Council provided printouts of all grants awarded for the funding years 1986-7 to 1994-5 for writing for performance.

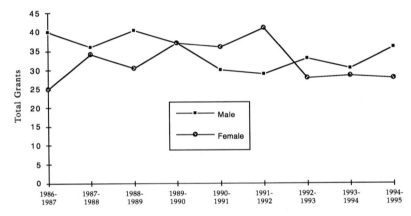

Figure 3: Literature Board Grants for writing for performance by Gender 1986-1995.

Figure 3 demonstrates the division of grants for writing for performance by gender from the Literature Board of the Australia Council from 1986/87 -1994/95. Fluctuations are attributable to policy decisions and the variety and quality of applications. It is interesting to note an overall gradual improvement in the position of women writers. There are some differences between years in relation to distribution by gender. In particular, there is a disparity between grants to men and women in last year's allocation, which we discuss later in the section.

Figure 4 (Literature Board Grants for writing for performance 1986-1995) breaks down Literature Board grants for writing for performance into different categories by the gender of recipients over the period 1986/87 - 1994/95 . Women writers began the period at a disadvantage in terms of representation. Most categories show reasonable equity in distribution over the years with some exceptions. Category B and Category A Fellowships show women as under represented. In earlier years women writers as individuals did not apply in as great numbers as men for these individual grants. Playwrights in Residence show women with an advantage in representation. The commissioning category also shows a reasonable rise in the number of women receiving grants. In particular, community theatre groups have given women the chance to explore and practice their skills within the company's own artistic agenda.

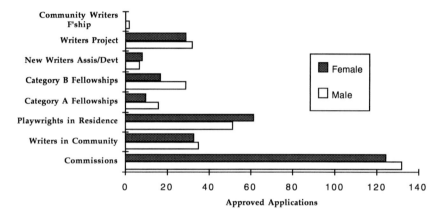

Figure 4: Literature Board Grants for writing for performance 1986-1995.

The rate of Commissioning grants is fairly equitable over the ten year period. The Australia Council was able to supply broad statistics on both applications and approvals for the years at the beginning and end of the cycle. Figure 5 Commission applications - 1986/87 compared with 1984/95 details applications and approvals of Commissions by gender in 1986/87 compared to 1994/95.

Our analysis shows some interesting divergences. Overall the number of applications and approvals have both increased, but more for men than for women. But proportions have not changed. In 1986/87 55% of the applicants were men and they had a 68% approval rate. Women applicants were 45% and they received 32% of that year's allocation. In 1994/95 men were 54% of total applicants and they received 63% of the grant money while women represented 46% of all applications and were successful at the rate of 37%. The Literature Board indicates that the lower commission approvals, from a committee with strong female representation, presumably reflected the quality of applications. It is surprising considering the widely held perception that the Australia Council is likely to be sympathetic to applications for commissions on behalf of women writers that over the nine year period shown that there has been only the most marginal increase in the percentage of commissions that involve women, even though, as we see in the next section, companies may believe that they are favouring women.

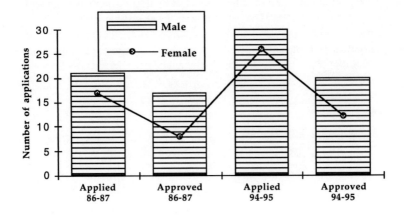

Figure 5: Commisioning applications - 1986/87 compared with 1994/95.

We noted in our discussion of Figure 3 that 1994-5 was aberrant in that more grants were approved for men than for women, and that this went against the general move towards a more equitable distribution. The major difference in fact occurred in the allocation of writer's project grants. As can be seen in Figure 6, more women than men applied yet fewer women than men were approved.

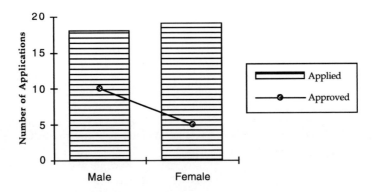

Figure 6: Writers' Project Grants 1994/95.

Women's access to development support

Gaining access to individual funding for projects and commissions is only part of the story. As women writers have indicated, for writers for performance there is a crucial reliance on development and workshopping organisations and networks.

The role of Playworks as a development organisation has been described in the Introduction. But we are certainly not alone. The Australian National Playwrights Centre (ANPC) is Australia's leading development institution for playwrights. Katharine Brisbane indicates

Through the 70s the only nationally-known women among the playwrights writing were Dorothy Hewett and Alma de Groen; and the overwhelming majority of new writers workshopped at the National Playwrights' Conference from 1973 were men.

It is important to note, that over the last ten years, the ANPC has increased its assistance to women writers. From 1985-1988, under the Artistic Directorship of Anne Harvey, the workshopping of plays by women at the annual Playwrights' Conference went from 2 out of 11 plays in 1985, to 6 out of 13 in 1986, 8 out of 19 in 1987 (four of these received readings only): in 1988, 6 of the 14 plays workshopped at the Conference were by women. Figures for the next two years are unavailable. In 1991, only 3 out of 10 plays workshopped were by women, and in 1992, 3 out of 11. Since 1993, under the directorship of May-Brit Akerholt, approximately 50% of all plays workshopped have been written by women. An ANPC survey in 1993 showed that only about 30% of the plays sent were by women, yet 50% of the selected Conference playwrights were women. May-Brit Akerholt says:

I have never had any problem finding plays by women that interest me. Whether this is because I am a woman, I've no idea. I don't actually think so - but it may have something to do with an awareness of potential, looking for the potential for creativity, rather than the final product. I would never choose a woman's play 'for the sake of it'; I would never choose a play by a female writer if it was inferior to that of a male writer. I don't believe in actively discriminating, but in being conscious of the general disparity of female/male representation when selecting works. But I am aware of the need to be supportive of female writers whose craft and experience may be somewhat lacking, but who have undoubted talent, ideas and creative vision. I do think we often reject works because they may not be 'finished' without recognising that the writer has what it takes although they may lack the practical craft or the actual experience needed to take the work to the next stage without support. This happens more often to female playwrights, because they have not been allowed to get the experience of working in the theatre, working with a team, which is what playwriting is all about.

May-Brit Akerholt sees the proportion of women's writing linked to the proportion of women in creative positions:

As for female directors, there's a big problem. It's getting smaller by the

year, but it'll take a long time before the imbalance is redressed. Again, we've got to look at the reasons why. In the decades which saw the real rise of Australian drama — or Australian theatre, we should say — there were very few women actually working in the industry. It takes time to train and get experience and get accepted on a professional level, and proportionally, the top quality female directors were largely out-numbered by males. I do not think there were so few female directors for such a long time simply because they were overlooked. Has anyone researched how many trained female directors there are compared to male? Would an un-trained or un-experienced male director, for instance, get better opportunities than a trained and experienced female director? Also, what's the ratio of female/male directing students over the last few years in the training institutions? Is there a discrimination there?

Do we need to lobby the institutions, or encourage the women to apply if the ratio shows that there are fewer women? As I am not aware of any (conscious or unconscious) gender discrimination by the theatre companies in choosing directors, it's hard to say what to do. They're offering work to directors with a track record — and there are too few women with a track record. In the last few years, several female directors have been given the opportunity to get that experience by the larger companies, such as Marion Potts, Melissa Bruce, Kim Durban, Rose Clemente, Cath McKinnon, Angela Chaplin, and many more. We need to ensure that these opportunities continue to be offered, so in a few years time, there will be just as many female directors with the same experience and respect as male directors.

She ponders whether women gravitate to particular roles in theatre.

There is a very high proportion of female dramaturgs in this country. Again, why? Are they the better dramaturgs for certain reasons? There are more female graduates in arts courses at university, and dramaturgs often have an academic background, for instance. Or are dramaturgs seen as 'inferior' in the hierarchy of theatre professionals, and so it's easier to employ them as dramaturgs, and the women think that it's easier to get jobs as dramaturgs, as it's not the 'top' position, so they are drawn to that?

The ANPC is often a route to getting plays on the stage. In early years writers such as Alma de Groen have had plays go on to full productions. Peta Tait's *Wallflowering* was a great success. In 1994 Beatrix Christian's play *Blue Murder* was given a production in the subscription season at Belvoir St. Theatre after workshopping at the 1993 Playwrights' Conference. Vanessa Bates' *Darling Oscar* had a production at New Stages, STC. Akerholt comments:

I do not think that a good play has less chance of being produced if it is by a woman rather than a man. There are some who would say, however, that because most artistic directors are male, they tend to choose male plays because they relate more to them. I think this is a very complex issue which cannot easily be answered. I don't think I necessarily relate more to a play by a woman than to one by a man. Do men relate better to Ibsen, Chekhov, Gow, Sewell, than women? Why did Katherine Thomson have a male dramaturg on Diving for Pearls *if he couldn't possibly relate as well to it as a woman could?*

We do not want to encourage more mediocrity, so in my opinion the question is how to ensure that the truly talented writers, male or female, are identified, encouraged, nurtured, and given every opportunity. What we must work towards is more women in the decision-making positions in theatre. There are a few already, and the last couple of decades have seen a big change in this respect, in the theatre companies and play development organisations, in the Australia Council, and in ministries for the arts around the country.

Getting works published

Australia's most important performing arts publisher is Currency Press. Currency Press has published a large number of plays and theoretical works by women writers including: *Converging Realities: Feminism in Australian Theatre* by Peta Tait, *Dorothy Hewett, The Feminine as Subversive* by Margaret Williams and *Its a Joke, Joyce: Australia's Funny Women* by Wendy Harmer. Currency's playlist includes a significant representation of plays by women; these include *Vocations/Going Home, The Rivers of China* and *The Girl Who Saw Everything* by Alma De Groen, *Dinkum Assorted* by Linda Aronson, *Diving for Pearls* by Katherine Thomson, *The Forty Lounge Cafe* by Tes Lyssiotis, *Hotel Sorrento* and *Falling from Grace* by Hannie Rayson, *Mummy Loves You, Betty Ann Jewell* by Susan Hawley, *Roses in Due Season/Bleedin' Butterflies* by Doreen Clarke, *The Serpent's Fall* by Sarah Cathcart, *Table for One* by Claire Haywood, *The Passion....* by Sue Ingleton, *The History of Water* by Noelle Janacewska, *The Glass Mermaid* by Tobsha Learner, *Blue Murder* by Beatrix Christian, *The Gap* by Anna Broinowski and *Wallflowering* by Peta Murray. It is heartening to note that in their forthcoming publications there are a high proportion by women: Jill Shearer's *The Family*, Elaine Acworth's *Composing Venus*, Hilary Bell's *Fortune,* Peta Murray's *Spitting Chips,* Joanna Murray-Smith's *Honour,* Margaret Kirby's *My Body My Blood* and Tes Lyssiotis's *Three Greek Australian Plays* will all be published in late 1995.

Playworks is impressed that Currency is seeking out quality plays whether or not these have had mainstage productions. Their entrepreneurial initiative in producing scripts for the program of first productions is also commendable. Katharine Brisbane indicates that this has involved the efforts of both individual women and also development organisations:

> *In the 1990s, thanks to the efforts of Playworks and other writers' theatres, and the growing maturity of the Australian theatre, writers like Hannie Rayson, Katherine Thomson, Tes Lyssiotis, Debra Oswald, Eva Johnson, Joanna Murray-Smith, Tobsha Learner, Robyn Archer and Heather Nimmo are working nationally and winning awards for their work. Complete equality is still a distance away; but the progress since the 1960s has been remarkable.*

f o u r

reports from states and territories

Playworks was interested in what changes there had been in the past ten years for women writers in getting their works performed, making the transition from page to stage (or community hall, warehouse or interactive media setting). Had any works by women been particularly notable or successful, financially or critically? What reasons could companies who had a small proportion of women's work give to explain this, and what ideas did they have as to how we could develop a higher proportion of women's writing in their programs?

We contacted all performing arts companies funded by the Australia Council and the state arts ministries in 1994-5. Our researchers in each state collected or developed questionnaires from 111 performing arts companies. Some of these were completed by researchers based on statistics from companies which had not responded and defunct companies. We asked the researchers in each state to give their own impressions of the situation.

All the researchers reported problems in getting statistics, difficulties in finding sources and even with figures provided by the companies themselves many gaps due to incomplete records. All statistics in this section can only be seen as indicative of trends.

from new south wales

The profile of women's work seems quite low within the companies with large resources, but high within the companies that run on the smell of an oily rag. Women's writing seems to be treated as a special interest option by resourced companies, where little if any is included in the yearly programme, but a 'Festival' of woman's writing will focus attention and profile on the company for a short period. Over the years, Sydney Theatre Co, Belvoir Street Theatre and Griffin Theatre Co have produced several series of short works written and directed by women.

Tanya Gerstle

The Companies:

The survey is based on information from 27 companies:

Sydney Theatre Company(STC); Company B/Belvoir St. Theatre; Marian St Theatre; Griffin Theatre; Q Theatre; Theatre South; Hunter Valley Theatre Company; Riverina Theatre Company; New England Theatre Company;

Sidetrack; Theatre of the Deaf; Legs on the Wall; Sydney Front; Theatre of Image; Death Defying Theatre (DDT); Etcetera; Open City; Witch Theatre; Party Line; Blue Squid Productions; Pact Theatre; Shopfront Theatre for Young People; 2 till 5 Youth Theatre; Freewheels Theatre in Education. Partial statistics were collected on, but no interviews were held with the following: Ensemble Theatre; Auto da Fe; Entr'acte.

No responses were received from REM; Northern Rivers Performing Arts; Australian Theatre for Young People; ACT; Sydney Mosaic Theatre; Frumpus; Zeal; Powerhouse Youth Theatre.

What proportion of work, over the past 10 years, has been written by women?

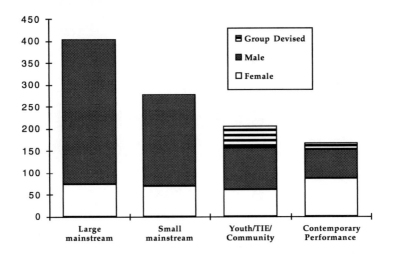

Figure 7: NSW - Comparison of works written by women

In looking more closely at the questionnaires from the companies, we can see that in the larger mainstream companies 1/5 (74) works were written by women and 86 were directed by women. Small mainstream and regional companies produced 1/4 (69) written by women and 48 were directed by women. In Youth/TIE/Community 1/3 (60) were written by women (49 were group devised) and 44 were directed by women. Contemporary Performance groups produced 1/2 (87) written by women (14 were group devised); 56+ were directed by women, 15 were group directed and 24 co-directed.

Overall, less than one third of works, broadly defined across the board, were written by women. A similarly low proportion were directed by women. Over the ten year period, however, in some companies there has been a small but steady increase in the work performed which is written by women, with a comparatively high proportion in contemporary performance work.

In the larger performing arts groups which present works on major stages and which receive the bulk of government funding, women are relatively poorly represented. The largest of these is the Sydney Theatre Company (STC). The STC provided statistics which show an uneven progression. In 1985, 6 out of their 22 plays were written by contemporary Australian women (and only two written by contemporary Australian men). In 1990 and 1991 no plays by contemporary Australian women were performed, although they wrote 2 out of 19 plays in 1993. In 1994, there were 2 plays by Australian women, and 12 by Australian men, out of 21. These figures, however, include all plays produced by the STC, including their main subscription season, schools plays, and their more innovative companies such as New Stages and Australian People's Theatre. Women writers have been less represented in the main subscription season. The STC has in recent years tried to encourage women writers. Playreadings, writers' forums, affiliated writers and solicited manuscript schemes and playwrights' residencies are all strategies which the STC has used. Writers whose work has been assisted by these initiatives include Beatrix Christian, Catherine Zimdahl, Donna Abela, Suzanne Spunner, Elaine Acworth, Vanessa Bates and Anna Maria Dell'Oso.

Other mainstage companies have smaller houses. Belvoir St. and its Company B board indicate in their response that they "are very conscious of male/female balance on its artistic board and in its programming". Belvoir is also involving other theatre groups from the performance and site-specific tradition in its development of a huge ex-railway workshop at Wilson St.

Colleen Chesterman reflects on this:

> *Writing up this survey reminds me that statistics are not so simple to analyse as they may appear. I am most familiar with the operations of Belvoir Street Theatre, where I was a member of the Company B Board, the Belvoir production house, between 1989 and 1992. I realised that the statistics for Belvoir St included outside hirings for both theatres, so that statistics include not only many companies in Downstairs Theatre (100) but also Upstairs (300) hires, which include the Gay and Lesbian Mardi Gras. These would increase the number of works by women, many self-producing. However, the main use for Upstairs is as a venue for the subscription season of Company B. Figures for Belvoir St. would have been more cohesive if they had reflected only the Company B subscription season.*

> *Company B, with a number of women on the Board and in key artistic positions, has been committed to encouraging women writers: over the*

past ten years Company B has shown Jenny Kemp's Call of the Wild,
Katherine Thomson's Diving for Pearls *and* Barmaids, *Robyn Archer's*
Cafe Fledermaus, *and Beatrix Christian's* Blue Murder. *But the
proportion rarely gets above 25%. I know from my time on Company B
how many factors can influence choice of plays and we are dealing with
seasons of only 5-6 works. We had other commitments as well as women
writers: to represent the best quality Australian works; to encourage new,
innovative theatrical styles; to bring works from Aboriginal writers or
companies; to include works which reflect Australia as a multi-cultural
society and to encourage women as directors. Preparing the program
was, as I am sure it is for other companies, a matter of finding the best
balance between these objectives, while also ensuring availability of plays,
directors etc. The situation is also complicated when, as was the case at
Belvoir, a couple of shows have not had good box office. In the straitened
circumstances in which many companies operate, one or two financial
failures means that risks may not be taken, that planned shows are
cancelled, that cast sizes are restricted and that shows which are likely to
be successful are brought in. These of course may be written by women,
but more often are by a chap called Bill Shakespeare and on the school
syllabus!*

*One final point. In 1982, Company B decided to encourage women
directors with a special season. We selected three women who were
interested in directing: Monica Pelizzari from film, Aboriginal performer
Kath Fisher and actor Lynette Curran and planned a three play season
downstairs. All three wanted to do plays written by women, and in the end
three unperformed plays were chosen. Jennifer Compton's* Julia's Song
was already a polished work, but both Cathy Craigie's Koori Love *and
Sue Woolf's* Painted Woman *were still being developed during the
production period. Fortunately both plays went on to have further
development and other performances, but it did indicate how a positive
action for one group who have had an historic disadvantage may also
involve action on behalf of other groups which may make its final success
very hard work. It should also be noted that these plays went on as a
series outside the main subscription season and in the smaller Downstairs
Theatre. Like many seasons of women's work, marginalised.*

Griffin has a commitment to new Australian work. Artistic Director Ros Horin
states

*We have actively sought out works by women writers and actively
commissioned new works by women ... Despite this the production
statistics do not reflect society's gender balance. It is a direction Griffin
will continue to try and remedy.*

In fact Griffin's subscription seasons over the past five years show 13 works by women, out of 33 shows, the bulk in seasons of short plays.

The Ensemble and Marian St. rely heavily on box-office rather than government support. Both have had small proportions of women's work. Marian St. indicates it is locked into a subscription season and argues that it does not have the money for development or dramaturgy, which they feel should be enforced on the largely funded companies.

Regional companies serve a local area in NSW, but may be linked with other companies for touring programs. In these small mainstage houses the proportion of women's work is low, varying between 20% and 25%. Theatre South however has 33% of its productions by women and estimates that 66% of its commissions have been for women in both mainstage and school projects: it was here that Katherine Thomson began her writing career. Riverina Theatre Company notes that in recent years women writers have come "more to the forefront" and have been included in seasons.

There is a larger proportion of women writing for the small companies primarily set up to either work with, or for, young people, and in community based companies. Such companies include Pact, which indicates that it "has had a pretty good track record for employing women creative artists, although the Board has been heavily male-dominated". Shopfront works through playbuilding; it estimates 33% of scripts in the last year have been by women, and hopes to increase the proportion. It indicates:

...plays by women invariably have very good roles for women; generally women write well for both genders, whereas male writers have female roles which (can be) very stereotyped and uninteresting.

Women are well represented in those companies set up by the performer/creators to make their own work. Within contemporary performance practice, where the methods of working are most often collaborative, the groups tend to have a gender balance. Open City refers to the women participants as equal partners, and encourages participating artists to extend their skills to include writing. They supported Dina Panozzo to develop and tour a solo performance *Varda che Brutta ... Poretta*. Legs on the Wall, a physical performance group, indicate that they employ the person they see best fits the job, with the current objective of keeping 50% artists female; they note:

We have had both good and bad experiences with works that have been written by women. I don't think it was a gender issue ... in any creative process there will be individual dynamics and positive and negative aspects.

Sydney Front utilised found texts but in two shows used specifically created texts by a woman Micky Furuya; her writing was chosen for "its relevance to our working methods and aesthetic not because of her sex". There are also special interest groups comprised totally of women, such as The Party Line and Witch; the latter, producing between 1 to 5 productions annually, states:

> *How thrilling it is to see original works by women, particularly lesbians, up on stage! One whinge though, where are all the scripts? It is very difficult to secure original works by Australian lesbians.*

Which works by women have been particularly notable?

Works which were seen as either critically successful or popular include *Barmaids* and *Diving For Pearls* by Katherine Thomson, which were both produced by Company B and which have since toured or been mounted by a number of other companies, including regional theatres and the Q Theatre; the reviews by Rosemary Neill of *The Australian* of these plays were highly critical.

The STC has had great success with *Hotel Sorrento* by Hannie Rayson, and particularly with *Two Weeks With The Queen* an adaptation by Mary Morris which has toured extensively, including a London season. Morris's *All of Me* was successful for Legs on the Wall, in thirteen seasons nationally and internationally. For Griffin Theatre there have been a number of successful hirings, including Dina Panozzo's *Varda che Bruta ... Poretta* which received Playworks dramaturgical assistance. In Griffin's own subscription seasons there have been successful works by a number of women writers in seasons such as *Shorts at the Stables;* there is particular excitement about the season of short plays *Passion*, all written by women, performed in 1994 and to be televised on SBS in 1995.

Regional theatres mentioned as successes *Lipstick Dreams* by Helen O'Connor and Simon Hopkinson, *Table For One* by Claire Haywood and a few years ago *Farewell Brisbane Ladies* by Doreen Clarke. Death Defying Theatre had an enormous local success in Fairfield with Noelle Janaczewska's *Blood Orange*; and Janaczewska has recently acted as dramaturg with Pact Theatre and Melina Marchetta on the dramatization of her prize-winning book *Looking for Alibrandi*. Another current youth theatre success is *Toxic Girls* by Mardi McConnochie, which 2 Till 5 is bringing back for a return season. A number of theatres, including the Q and the now-defunct Toetruck, mentioned their success with *Dags* by Debra Oswald. Sydney Front's Clare Grant had a great success with *Woman in the Wall,* written by Mickey Furuya; Furuya received the NSW Premier's award for best writing for theatre for her part in the group-devised work *First and Last Warning*. Open City are another group whose collaborative projects, with strong female input from co-director Virginia Baxter and other women contributors, have had considerable critical success. Theatre of the Deaf are excited by their recent production *The Sign of the Phantom,* the first original deaf musical, written by Melissa Reeves. The women's theatre group The Partyline is closely associated with Melbourne group Club Swing, whose piece *Appetite* was a hit at the 1995 Edinburgh Festival.

Are women working in key creative roles?

Over the ten year period women have occupied key creative positions in a number of the companies. Currently there are women artistic directors at Griffin Theatre Co (Ros Horin), Pact Theatre Co (Anna Messariti), Ensemble Theatre Co (Sandra Bates), Blue Squid Productions (Di Johnson), Shopfront (Maryanne Braggs), Theatre of the Deaf (Julia Cotton, previously Carol-Lee Aquiline) and at Belvoir Street Theatre where the General Manager has always been a woman and where the Company B Board, which makes artistic decisions, has always had a number of women directors including actors Lindy Davies, Gillian Hyde and Kerry Walker, administrators Maureen Barron, Sue Hill, Liz Mullinar and Barbara Bridges. Over the past ten years women have also been in key creative positions at the Q (which Doreen Warburton founded and where Michelle Fawdon is now a trainee AD), Death Defying Theatre, Etcetera and Sidetrack.

There have been Writers-in-residence/Dramaturgs at Theatre South, Sydney Theatre Co, Griffin Theatre Co, Pact, Theatre of the Deaf, DDT, Freewheels, Belvoir Street Theatre, and Legs On The Wall. Witch Theatre Inc and The Partyline are both companies set up and run by women. Legs On The Wall, Sidetrack Performance Group, Etcetera, Entr'acte, 2 till 5 Youth Theatre, Sydney Front and Open City are companies of performer/creators, which mostly devise their works in collaboration with other artists. Entr'acte and Open City are companies co-directed by women. In these companies there seems to be either a gender balance, or more female artistic personnel involved. All members share creative, performing and administrative tasks.

Some companies made strong statements in their surveys about their policies for women. Companies that have a current policy of gender equity or try to create gender balance within key artistic personnel are Open City, Legs On The Wall, Griffin Theatre Co, Belvoir Street Theatre Co and DDT.

Griffin Theatre Company employed women in most of the key creative roles for their 1995 Festival of New Works: Artistic Director, Festival Director, Co-Director, Dramaturgical Consultant; it is interesting to note, however, that only two out of seven plays in the festival were written by women.

What are the reasons given if there is a low proportion of women's work?

The Sydney Theatre Company is aware of the issues involved. They were one of the companies involved in the Australia Council affirmative action pilot program and have increased the number of women in key creative roles in the company. They acknowledge a problem in their repertoire:

> *As a state theatre company STC has a responsibility to produce plays from the classical repertoire, as well as plays from the recent international repertoire, alongside Australian work. Given that the classical repertoire has few plays by women, this means a statistical bias towards plays by men, often dead.*

We're assured this is not a plug for their most recent touring success.

Marian St does not produce new plays, relying instead on trusted successes to suit its "middle-class North Shore audience". They can't "gamble"; shows must be single-set, low cost. Unknown writers of either gender are seen as too much of a box office risk.

The Artistic Director of New England Theatre Company was well aware of and admired some contemporary women's writing, but said the subject matter was at times not appropriate for his audience (regional, middle class), and the cast sizes were too large for his budget.

Hunter Valley Theatre Company administration suggests that choice of repertoire is dependent largely on who the Artistic Director knows and wants to work with. Therefore if the Artistic Director is a man he is more likely to select new works written by men and established works that he identifies with, which are most often written by men. If the Artistic Director is a woman, or the male Artistic Director has creative advisers who are women, it is much more likely that a play written by a woman will be included in a subscription season or program of work.

All companies, not including those that consciously seek women's writing or have a gender equity policy, maintain strongly that gender is irrelevant to their selection of material or director. They state that the works produced are chosen to appeal to their audience, and the directors are the best people for that particular piece.

What suggestions do companies offer to improve the situation?

Sydney Theatre Company has committed itself to the process of commissioning writers. Currently four out of six are women.

> *This indicates a desire to increase the number of quality plays written by women and so then to increase the production of plays by women.*

Many companies stated that they have no resources to process unsolicited scripts.

One of these, Belvoir Street, indicated that exposure of women's writing in the form of readings and workshopped scripts was essential. By exposure they were referring to the holding of festivals of new works in the houses of all established companies. Belvoir has hosted a couple of events for emerging writers including *Girl's Night Out*, a series of short works. The likelihood of creative personnel attending such an event if it is on their premises is high.

> *The major factor in the production of women's writing is that it has to be heard or seen. Any initiative by women writers or Playworks that provides a facility for the writer to be around the theatre and is designed to fit in with the priorities of a particular theatre would be welcome. The company cannot stretch its already overloaded resources.*

Griffin hosts a Festival of New Works. It states:

> *We have enjoyed terrific artistic and box office success with works written by women and will continue to actively promote the work of women writers.*

Riverina states that they are:

> *...becoming increasingly conscious of the need to produce plays by women. As far as the audience is concerned they seem not to discern or hold an opinion about who writes the play.*

Death Defying Theatre are always:

> *...seeking writers who are interested in creating work in a context involving community. We are also proactively seeking to work with writers who are of non English-speaking backgrounds.*

Open City emphasises:

> *...the open collaborative approach and the long development process encourages women in new ways of writing ... Even writing for solo performance is an intensively collaborative process, important for finding different ways for women to write.*

2 Till 5 Youth Theatre already actively encourages young women writers as it is a youth company whose membership is predominantly female. They are looking at the work of woman prose writers to commission performance works, as they are constantly in need of subject matter that speaks to and about young women.

from victoria

Drama funding in Victoria has gone from $1,750,700 in 84/85 to $2,187,000 in 93/94. This is a very low increase in ten years. It peaked in 89/90. Very little funding from the Drama Board goes to individuals: only 2-3 per year recieved grants. The Literature Board of the Victorian Ministry for the Arts has been more supportive of playwrights' development.

I waded through files about withdrawing support to various dying companies, particularly community based ones. I noticed that regular and unquestioned funds still went to local philharmonic orchestras rather than visiting artists or innovative community arts programs.

Small noises in the distance!

There is a Women Directors Group in Melbourne which exists as needed support network. There is amongst the members a healthy ongoing debate about whether they can support women in theatre without supporting women writers and whether or not there are differences in gender aesthetics.

The Media Entertainment and Arts Alliance has had a Women's Committee for over 7 years. They are starting a campaign that looks at the quantity and quality of roles for women in television and the federal office is in the process of forming an agreement with the ABC regarding gender and race casting breakdowns. While this doesn't affect directly women playwrights, it is another avenue open to us in terms of possible action. Often women create more substantial and satisfying roles for women actors and perhaps the MEAA is interested in addressing theatre companies along these lines.

Jennie Swain

The Companies

The survey is based on information from 18 companies:

Melbourne Theatre Company; Playbox; La Mama; Melbourne Writers' Theatre; Melbourne Workers' Theatre; Australian Contemporary Theatre Company; Arena; Handspan; Hildegard; St. Martin's Theatre; Oxford Children's Theatre Trust; OPA; Chameleon; Crying in Public Places; Crying out Loud; Soup Kitchen Theatre; Chamber-Made Opera; Back to Back.

These 16 companies include 2 major and well-funded companies, and a mixture of youth theatre, community based theatre, companies committed to development of new Australian work and some experimental performance companies, although most experimental work is developed by individuals such as Lyndal Jones.

The following companies were substantially funded but are now defunct. It was possible to identify some information through the Victoria Ministry for the Arts files but no details of productions or personnel: Anthill; The Mill Theatre; West (did have mainly women Artistic Directors. The bulk of their work was group devised); Woolly Jumpers.

Groups approached with no response: Going Through Stages (Peter King, currently unfunded): Gilgul Theatre (Barrie Kosky has been quoted as saying "Writers' theatre is dead"); Desoxy (almost purely physical theatre).

No contact was made because of time constraints with Murray River Performing Group; $5 Theatre Company (very small but have commissioned works from a few local women writers); Whistling in the Theatre (now defunct. Produced a substantial amount of work, mainly group devised).

What proportion of work, over the past ten years, has been written by women?

In Melbourne there are two big companies: Playbox and Melbourne Theatre Company (MTC), a handful of smaller companies producing regular work and a number of small project based companies. Many of the companies committed to community theatre have lost their funding in the last five years.

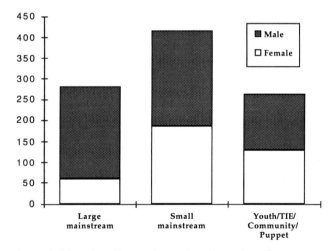

Figure 8: Victoria - Comparison of works written by women

Note: The Categories Small mainstream and Youth/ TIE/ Community/ Puppet include any group devised or collaborative works.

The proportion of works performed over the past ten years by women in Victoria has been tiny in the two main companies, at only 22%; this reflects 33% in Playbox and only 16% in MTC. Small mainstage companies reach 45% because of the very high number of works produced by La Mama and its commitment to women writers. In the community and youth field the proportion is almost 50%.

And what reasons are given for the low proportion of women's work? Poor quality, fear of taking financial risks, lack of understanding of the issue. Almost everyone steers away from the idea that there is a deliberate gender bias.

Melbourne Theatre Company

In 1985, one out of the MTC's 20 productions was written by a contemporary Australian woman. The situation improved dramatically in 1988 when three out of 20 were by women. Those heady days were quickly forgotten and MTC seems to have thought that any more than 2 plays by women a year would lose the company money. 1995 is a reckless year. MTC have programmed 5 plays by contemporary Australian women out of 21, 9 of which are by contemporary Australian writers, but four of these are short plays or collaborative works by women. Overall the MTC has produced 1/6 plays by women over the ten year period.

The selection of plays for programming currently goes through the dramaturg to the Repertoire Committee. This committee consists of the artistic director, (up to now always male), any associate directors (Robyn Nevin is currently an associate), the dramaturg (there has only ever been one female dramaturg with MTC and that was in the 70s), designer, production manager, education program representative and casting personnel who are often women.

Of the 150 or so unsolicited manuscripts that are received per year, *none* has ever been produced. Any worthwhile scripts are shown around so that the writers become known to key personnel.

In the last 7 years there have been 7 women directors: Jenny Kemp, Ros Horin, Robyn Nevin, Vicky Eagger, Gail Edwards, Mary Hickson and Kim Durban. Kim is now an Artistic Associate at Playbox. These directors did not necessarily work with women writers.

Of the 6 plays currently under commission by MTC, 4 are by women: Katherine Thomson, Pamela Leversha, Catherine Zimdahl and Dorothy Hewett. Two of these women have been supported by Playworks.

Successful productions at MTC by women writers have included *Blabbermouth* an adaptation by Mary Morris, *Sistergirl* by Sally Morgan, *The Girl Who Saw Everything* by Alma De Groen, *Diving for Pearls* by Kath Thomson and *The Sisters Rosensweig* by American Wendy Wasserstein.

Playbox

Playbox in its survey form indicates that over the last ten years it has not improved on figures of around 25% women playwrights in the main subscription season, though overall its figures suggest 1 play out of 3.

Their selection of plays comes from unsolicited scripts, commissions and development seasons such as *Theatre in the Raw*. Aubrey Mellor, current Artistic Director, creates a large short list, a panel of readers and artistic committee discuss the list and the Artistic Director makes the final decisions.

Aubrey Mellor, in a recent letter sent to the Literature Board and then to Playworks, indicates that he is most concerned by the low proportion of works written by women which are submitted to Playbox.

> *In my first year here only about 10% of all plays received by us were by women - 78 out of almost 800. In the next twelve months it seems to have dropped to about 8%.*

In the Asian Australian Playwrighting Competition 20 plays out of a total of 62 were from women (referred to by the Playbox respondent as "that 25% again").

Playbox indicates:

> *While Playbox attempts to follow a policy of 50% female productions, at this stage the quality of the scripts is such that this is not possible. As a result much of our commissioning and development program is geared to women.*

Mellor suggests somewhat ironically that Australia Council statistics showing relatively equal application rates for commissions and so on are not surprising.

> *It is well known that women are a priority area hence applicants know that applications for such might attract support.*

Playbox currently has 16 commissions in process of which 7 are women. Of the 1995 *Raw Works* program (to date) there have been 16 showcase productions of which 6 have been initiated by women.

Playbox productions by women which have been notable include *Hotel Sorrento* and *Falling From Grace* by Hannie Rayson, *Cafe Fledermaus* by Robyn Archer, *Love Child* by Joanna Murray Smith, *The Forty Lounge Cafe* by Tess Lyssiotis, *The Glass Mermaid* and *Wolf* by Tobsha Learner, *Nice Girls* by Linden Wilkinson and *Reginka's Lesson* by Linda Aronson.

Only half of these were directed by women. Playbox, in their response to the survey, made the point that "*even when given the option of choosing a director, most female playwrights do not choose exclusively female directors. While often male playwrights prefer female directors."*

Nonetheless their statistics show considerably less than 20% of their directors have been women.

Playbox considered how as a company they could redress the balance and suggested that Playworks:

> *...encourage writers to send Playbox their scripts;*
> *submit ideas for Theatre in the Raw;*
> *suggest names of suitable Victorian assessors; and*
> *work with Playbox on script workshops for Victorian writers.*

Aubrey Mellor indicates in addition that they are:

> *...actively attempting to redress this perceived problem by calling special meetings with women playwrights and by giving their plays special feedback and creating more workshops and 'tryout' presentations for women's material.*

Mellor also believes that something else needs to happen at earlier levels e.g. schools, university and CAE courses. In addition he points out:

> *Clearly much writing happens in leisure time and perhaps women have less, or are less selfish in prioritising it for themselves.*

Smaller Companies

Arena Theatre Company is a company geared towards young people and schools shows. It has been successfully funded during the last ten years during which time the percentage of works by women playwrights has ranged from 25% to 100% for the 1995 and 1996 program.

Rose Myers, the company's current Artistic Director writes:

> *Arena has had 3 women artistic directors and 2 men. In a small company, artistic vision is given by the artistic directors and this has a big impact on the statistics. Arena has employed more women than men in all areas; administrators, acrobats, writers, composers etc. 7 out of 11 board members are women. All of this has an influence and just shows how important it is to have Equal Opportunity policies in all aspects of company life.*

The company's three most critically acclaimed and financially successful projects have featured women in the traditionally male world: *The Women There* by Julianne O'Brien, *Electro Diva* by Anita Durton and *Fix it Alice* by Ernie Gray.

La Mama produces around 50 plays a year. The production package includes venue, publicity, directors' and writers' fees, some set and props and front of house. The door takings are shared by casts and crews. Generally playwrights are local and contemporary. Artistic directors have always been women. Most of the staff are women. La Mama is generally recognised as one of the most woman-friendly companies to survive in Australia. At one stage, when current AD Liz Jones felt there weren't enough works by women being presented, they created a special women's season to redress the balance. In 1995 La Mama has commissioned Chinese-Australian woman writer Ding Xiao-Qi.

Liz Jones says

> *It seems vital to me that there is a space like La Mama — neutral and nurturing — that allows a creative idea to leave the confines of the garrett, the campus, the studio or the ghetto and begin to function effectively in a general context, exposed to broad, intelligent audiences given good publicity and media reviews.*

Jones points out that the first play by a "living Australian woman" appeared at La Mama seven years after the theatre's birth in 1974. In 1975, 3 out of 11 plays were by women; by 1985, 7 out of 23. Now in 1995, the proportion is around 50%, and 50% are also directed by women.

Chamber-Made Opera indicates that:

> *...as an opera company we have an unprecedented history of presenting work written and composed by women. These works have been presented in small and large theatres; been toured and recorded for radio broadcast. We have engaged several women designers, one woman music director. We currently have a woman writer on a training program with the company.*

St. Martin's: The Victorian Centre for Youth Arts. The survey responses indicate that they are aware of the issues and that the gender mix is "pretty equitable". Statistics show however that only about 33% of the work produced is written by women.

Soup Kitchen Theatre is a small company that mainly produces lunchtime theatre in the city and is run by women. In their survey they state that they have "an affirmative action policy to try to employ or work with more female than male actors in any season". However, it seems that the affirmative action policy is not so effective in relation to writing. Over 5 years, less than 50% of their shows have been written by women.

Melbourne Workers Theatre since 1987 has usually had a female Artistic Coordinator. More than half of their productions have been written by women and directed by women.

Handspan Theatre produces sophisticated puppet/illusion/visual theatre. Their survey states that "precedence is given to the idea submitted rather than by whom." Only 33% of their projects have been credited to a woman writer.

Melbourne Writers Theatre stopped producing plays in 1991 and concentrated on dramaturgy. All dramaturgs have been male, although women have applied and the panel that makes the decisions is predominantly female. Generally male writers dominate, however their female administrator says, "Our best new writers are female".

from south australia

There has been some very good work by women in South Australia over the past five years. I think there is more a sense here of writers full-stop being marginalised, rather than female writers in particular. It really is no easier for male South Australian writers to crack the top levels than it is for female.

Where there is consistent commissioning and development of new work (namely, in all areas bar the State Theatre Company level) there is essentially equality of opportunity between male and female writers, However, most companies are seriously underfunded and this situation is likely to remain and, perhaps, worsen, so few are going to take risks on emerging writers. This is probably the major area of concern in this state. (For example, there are rumours as I write of a possible forced amalgamation of Patch Theatre Company and two theatre companies for young people which are both successful, both get good box office, target very different audiences and use very different performance styles. It's a bankrupt funding sensibility that would even contemplate such a move.)

What is lacking is the developmental input that would promote more than the occasional piece of work on a national level. Looking at the broad range of work produced by South Australians (men as well as women) I would say that over the past five to ten years, it has, commensurate with the population base, achieved a national quality, but, when that has happened, it has rarely been seen elsewhere. It remains difficult for writers to achieve a national profile, to be in a position to earn a real living from their artistic work from S.A. It is much more sensible to pursue productions interstate where there are the skills and will to be put at the service of a work-in-progress.

That last point leads to the next one. A real problem in recent years anyway is that there has been lacking here the dramaturgical expertise to help bring writers of seemingly average talent up to the 'good' level and writers of the 'good' level to the capacity where their work may occasionally be seen as extraordinary. Theatre is a very complex art. To succeed at first production, which seems to be a demand in Australia, requires ongoing and long-term commitment to development. However it would take major vision to initiate a coherent developmental program in South Australia at the moment because to do so would require a real understanding of the way creativity works. And an acknowledgment that it would take time, even if only because it has been neglected for a long period. A program of Masterclasses initiated by the Department for the Arts has gone some way towards redressing the worst of the imbalance but what is lacking is a thoughtful, structured long-term commitment, without which the development of what talent there is must necessarily remain ad hoc and intermittent. The will for this does not seem to exist, certainly at political levels. For this reason, I think it is unlikely to happen.

Verity Laughton

The Companies

The survey is based on material from 17 companies:

State Theatre Company of South Australia; Vitalstatistix; Living Voice, Theatro Oneiron; Doppio Teatro; Red Shed; Jumbuck Youth Theatre; Unley Youth Theatre; Riverland Youth Theatre; Magpie Youth Theatre; Junction Theatre; Patch Theatre; Mainstreet Community Theatre; Mad Love; Carouselle; Port Youth Theatre; Big Ensemble.

Partial information was gained from Backstares and Theatre Guild.

No responses were received from Theatre of Hell, Reckless Moments, Paperbags, Reincarnated Bills, Umbrella House.

What proportion of work, over the past ten years, has been written by women?

If you look across the range of companies that have been operating in SA over the past ten years the statistics regarding the proportion of plays written by women are fairly healthy in certain areas.

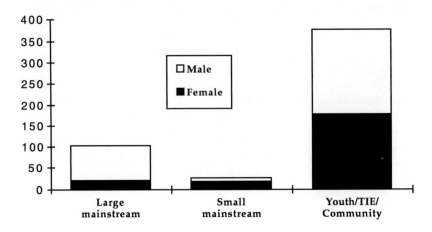

Figure 9: Comparison of works written by women

There are ten companies in the community and youth area (all of which are still operating) where the proportion of work by women is 50% or better. This easily balances those companies (such as Jumbuck and Big Ensemble) where the statistics are much lower. In both these cases, too, the reason for the low proportion of works written by women would be happenstance rather than the operation of prejudice, unconscious or otherwise, The founder of Jumbuck, for example, was Dave Brown (now Artistic Director at Patch). He wrote the bulk of their early work, he happens to be male. Big Ensemble has traditionally performed classics, but is now considering a change of direction and commissioning a woman. This is more than balanced, however by the fact that the increasingly successful Vitalstatistix Theatre Company, for example, has 100% women writers and will continue to do so. It is also noticeable that in most companies the balance has improved over recent years (e.g. Unley Youth, Riverland Youth to name just two.) Magpie shows that 45% of its work is by women writers, and more done collaboratively. Doppio Teatro has had a strong influence from its founder Teresa Crea in devising and writing work. Red Shed has 64% of its productions written by women.

The problem, where it arises, is at glass ceiling level. Both the Stage Company and Harvest Theatre Company (both of which are now out of business — is there a lesson in this?) predominantly produced work by established male writers in an effort to crack what were regarded as conservative audiences. With the best of stated intentions, the only really big gun in S.A., the State Theatre Company, has done the same.

Because of the STCSA's pre-eminent status this fact probably deserves a bit of attention. Despite an expressed desire on the part of successive Artistic Directors to promote the work of women, when you look at the statistics, the reverse, in fact, has happened, The figures consistently list 1 or 2 plays out of a season of 8 or 9 as being written by women. Even when there is a larger than usual number of plays written by contemporary Australian writers, this figure holds true. The STCSA is in an unenviable position. They are underfunded by the State government for what they have been given an express charter to do and, in the current economic climate (there is a doom mentality in S.A.) are expected to justify their existence in economic terms by showing results at the box office. There has also been an assumption that it is part of their brief to cover the canon of theatrical works, which is highly biased towards male writers. Therefore they must appeal to a conservative audience. Therefore adventures in development are minimal or short-lived. There are not many sure-bet box-office gold female writers in Australia. Therefore there is a reluctance to back the work of any writers bar those with a very strong track record. Catch 22 for female writers, a situation which is reflected in similar companies elsewhere in Australia.

Most recent artistic directors have done something to try to redress the situation. In fact, it is interesting to consider the statistics here. The period when most consistent attention was paid across the board to women theatre workers was John Gaden's period as Artistic Director, contrary to the impression in the theatre community. During that period, of ten plays written by contemporary Australian writers, four were by women, there was a female Company Dramaturg (Darrelyn Gunzberg) for a proportion of the time, Mary Moore was (and is) an influential designer and Gale Edwards co-directed three plays with Gaden before going on to direct another in her own right. We all know where that has led. Yet all those 'conservative' subscribers remember that time as subscriber-heaven. Perhaps that subscriber audience might not be so conservative after all!

Other artistic directors have also shown commitment. Simon Phillips, for example, scheduled female writers in 4 out of 6 plays in the *Quickies* series that STCSA ran in 1990. Chris Westwood, the current Executive Producer, has focused on bringing in female directors where possible. In response to the survey, she indicates that there have been "absolutely not enough plays by women over the past twenty years. My concern is that big subscription houses require big plays, big ideas from 'public' culture (read male)". Writers have already indicated that women will write big ideas, or that perhaps the definition of 'public' culture needs to be changed.

Which works by women have been particularly notable?

In creative terms (and trying to look at a cross-section of companies) the following works by women have been highlights.
At the STCSA Katherine Thomson's *Diving for Pearls* was very successful (more

so than the production of her play *Barmaids*) and, similarly, for Magpie, her *A Sporting Chance*, in 1987, went very well. *High Society*, adapted by Carolyn Burns, was both a critical and financial success for the STCSA: Peta Murray's *This Dying Business* for Junction Theatre Company was a great success. The Festival Centre entrepreneured Robyn Archer's *Akwanso, Fly South* and also brought the very successful *Pack of Women* by Archer to Adelaide. The Adelaide University Theatre Guild had a big success with *Ring the Bell Softly, There's Crepe On the Door* devised with an all female cast and directed by Sue Rider in 1988. Red Shed has had consistent success with seasons of *In Cahoots and Sweetown*, both by Melissa Reeves, Doppio Teatro has produced a number of works written by Teresa Crea, its co-founder and Artistic Director. Of these, *Red Like the Devil* has been probably the greatest success but several have done very well.

Some years ago, Troupe had success with Anne Brookman's *The Colour Keeper.* Unley Youth Theatre produced *Toxic Girls* by Mardi McConnochie, which went on to tour interstate, Patch Theatre Company (in co-production with the Adelaide Festival Centre Trust) has produced Gillian Rubenstein's *Space Demons* and *Galax Arena.* Vitalstatistix had great success with Roxxy Bent's *Florence Who?* Doreen Clarke's *Farewell Brisbane Ladies* was very successful for the STC at Theatre 62 in the mid-eighties.

Over the past few years Melissa Reeves, Mardi McConnochie and Roxxy Bent have developed as writers and moved interstate, primarily to further their careers. Carolyn Burns has also moved interstate. Andrea Lemon is now living in S.A and doing good work. (Lemon has a commission for the Adelaide Festival Centre Trust which has promoted a number of S.A writers, including some women, in its *Brave New Works* program. The Trust is quite important in developmental terms in South Australia because of its history of co-producing with companies like Patch Theatre Co, Red Shed and Doppio to help present works for which the companies alone would not have the budget. It is possible to make a living writing for theatre for young people/community theatre in South Australia — Anne Brookman, Gillian Rubenstein (who is primarily as writer of prose but whose theatre work has been very successful), Pat Rix and Kate O'Brien would fall into this category at least in the work they are doing at the moment. Darrelyn Gunzberg remains in S.A but has diversified into film and prose. She was also proactive enough to mount a production herself of her most recent play. Verity Laughton writes a cross-section of adult theatre, prose and video, Cath McKinnon writes, but works primarily as a director, same for Catharine Fitzgerald and Teresa Crea, Eva Johnson is writing again, Margie Fischer is now writing full-time. All these women are doing good work. Most of their work, when performed, has been successful. Some e.g., Melissa Reeves and Teresa Crea, have had pieces which have toured interstate. Doreen Clarke, unfortunately, no longer writes.

Are women working in key creative roles?

Some of the key women in creative positions are Doppio Teatro: Artistic Director, Teresa Crea; Mainstreet Theatre: Artistic Director, Mary McMenamin; Port Youth Theatre Workshop: Director Susan Ditter; Red Shed Theatre Company: Cath McKinnon, one of the two directors who work with the company; State Theatre Company: Executive Producer, Chris Westwood; Vitalstatistix: Artistic Director, Margie Fischer (Vitals is in the process of changing to being run as a production house for female creative artists and run by an all-female board); Living Voice — female collective.

Some companies, e.g. Backstares Theatre and Magpie Theatre, at present have no key female input but in the past have had (and, as likely as not, in the future may have again) strong female input.

Many of the theatre companies have female administrators, including Red Shed, Patch, Mainstreet, Theatre Guild, Magpie.

What are the reasons given if there is a low proportion of women's work?

Except at the top end, there is not in most companies an excessively low proportion of work by female writers being performed.

When work is new, and in the fields of theatre for young people, community theatre or puppet theatre, like Carouselle Theatre Company, there is a reasonably healthy balance between male and female writers.

Where a company has been established as a vehicle for female theatre workers (Vitalstatistix) or where there is a strong political base to the company (Red Shed, now, and Troupe in the past) there is a specific commitment to women's work.

Some companies, such as Mainstreet at present, have tended towards a bias towards women because of the individual artistic director's priorities. Other companies, like Doppio Teatro do have a commitment to gender balance. But, in terms of the evolution of the company, the main artistic thrust has come from Teresa Crea, who happens to be female. If she had been male the statistics could have gone in the opposite direction.

Theatro Oneiron explains that its three works by women writers have all been artistically good and well received by Greek-Australian audiences:

Female playwrights are not an unusual or rare phenomenon in modern Greek culture.

The question of male-female writer ratio does have relevance, however, in the area that is perceived as art and high-status art in particular. (Laughton indicates that she is not proposing these definitions: "all creative product should aspire to the status of art in my view and much of the work in more marginal areas should be seen as such").

Here then, where the economic imperative is highest (the STCSA and, in its day, The Stage Company), an attempt to reach gender-balance may be expressed but not in fact achieved. In the case of the current STCSA the reasons for not doing more work by women could probably be described as reluctant pragmatism. New work by women is seen as too risky except very occasionally. The STCSA has commissioned a new piece by Robyn Archer for 1996/7, this is the first since an (unsuccessful, primarily because under-developed) commission in 1992. The STCSA explains:

> *Most unsolicited scripts are by women. Some are very good. Because we have been unable to take financial risks, it has been difficult to use them because few women writers have a 'big name' we can market. We have been loathe to leave any season without a woman writer and have always found the experience of producing women's plays extremely positive.*

What suggestions do companies offer to improve the situation?

Most companies are keen to remain conscious of issues of gender equality in their programming. Where they felt it was impossible to actually formulate a policy it was usually their perception that they were being squeezed by conflicting imperatives.

In terms of a program of activity, the STCSA appears to have no explicit developmental policy, and thus no explicit commitment to develop work written by women. Work by women appears occasionally and almost opportunistically. Development may have been put in the too-hard basket. To a degree this is also an outcome of funding problems.

The only companies doing ongoing developmental work for writers of adult theatre are Vitalstatistix, Red Shed, Doppio and Junction. All of these except Red Shed (which by and large works from within the company) are specialist theatre companies. Living Voice, a project based company, wants to encourage more communication with playwrights, as it finds it difficult to contact new writers. Mainstreet Theatre does a lot of new work but little of this is seen in Adelaide. It is a community theatre:

> *...therefore we have people involved in our productions for who they are as opposed to what their gender, colour, shape or religion is.*

In the field of youth theatre there is more consistent use, including development, of women writers. Unley Youth Theatre, for example, commissions and develops.

Women writers are more likely to write strong roles for young women ... be more sensitive to concerns ... offer role models to young women of women as primary creators.

There is, however, almost no opportunity for writers to write a play that has its impetus in their own creative obsessions with any real expectation of eventually finding a production in their home state. Mostly if they are writing for commission they will be writing within guidelines. Verity Laughton sees these as a potential problem in that:

...many of these guidelines have arisen out of the fact that there is funding available to cover "art-with-a-social-function" but not art per se (although of course the artistic personnel within the companies will have their own artistic agendas within the guidelines of their companies).

from queensland

Playworks should be very aware of what is happening inside the institutions where theatrical practices are being taught. Many companies have been set up in Queensland by graduate students or staff from institutions such as Queensland University of Technology and James Cook University. These companies include: The House Is Live! TN! Tropic Line Theatre, Up North, Renegade Theatre and Grin & Tonic. Practitioners who teach at such institutions include dramaturgs Louise Gough and Hilary Beaton. It is important that students know about the work and the aims of Playworks.

Another trend is the willingness of companies to move across art forms and technologies. Snot Arts, for example, has moved away from purely performance-based work into video and visual arts. This is because many of the young people they work with are transient and cannot commit themselves to a rehearsal process. Contact Youth Theatre and Street Arts are currently building sites on World Wide Web: both of these companies consider these as creative projects. La Boite now holds an annual festival, *Shock Of The New*, which presents works which are challenging theatre form. The festival began last year and was largely successful.

The women interviewed tended to treat plays and visual texts as theatre, whereas the men tended to separate them out as Theatre and Performance Art. This area of definitions is one that Playworks is certainly positioned to comment upon.

There are opportunities for women writers and dramaturgs in Queensland and this is only the case because of organisations such as Playworks.

Clearly over the ten year period '85-95 there have been significant improvements. Hilary Beaton pointed out is that there is not enough long term development of writers: "Companies are too interested in developing new work. Wrong! They should be developing writers". This practice of going for the short fix rather than supporting a writer as a body of work evolves does have a particularly negative impact on women as their gaps between jobs are still significantly longer.

Josephine Fleming

The Companies.

The following 16 companies have been included in this survey:

Queensland Theatre Company (1985-95) and Brolgas TIE Company (1985-94); La Boite Theatre; Brisbane Repertory Theatre (1985-90); Twelfth Night Theatre (1985-95); Tropic Line, Townsville (1986-95); Just Us Theatre (Cairns based company) (1993-95); The House is Live! (1993-95); Renegade Theatre (1995); Rock & Roll Circus (1986-95); Kooemba Jdarra (1993-95); Icy Tea - Inala Community Theatre Inc (1986-95); Street Arts Community Theatre (1985-95); Contact Youth Theatre (1989-95); La Boite Youth Arts (1986-95); Snot Arts (formerly Slice of Ice Youth Theatre) (1988-95).

Companies with incomplete information are: Metaluna: New Moon (Townsville). Companies which did not respond were: Taking Liberties (Community Theatre Company); Grin & Tonic (exclusively performing Shakespeare); La Luna Youth Theatre (Townsville). Companies which have ceased operations and records not obtained: TN!

What proportion of work over the past ten years, has been written by women?

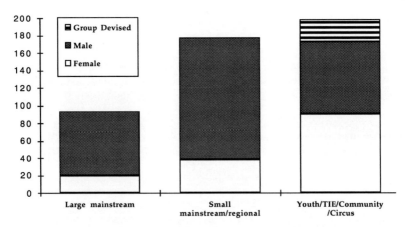

Figure 10: Queensland - Comparison of works written by women

There is a low proportion in the large mainstream company and a better situation in the smaller mainstream and regional companies. There is however effective equality in work in the community, theatre for young people, TIE and in physical performance. In addition it should be noted that of the 385 works presented over the ten year period: 228 (59%) were written by contemporary Australian writers; 99.5 (26%) were written by contemporary Australian women writers; 179 (46%) were directed by women and 58 (15%) were dramaturged by women. This latter statistic is a bit misleading as there was no question re numbers of total dramaturgs. In many companies there was often no dramaturg attached to a production. The number of dramaturgs used by companies has increased markedly in the last four years.

Queensland Theatre Company (QTC) has dramatically increased its performance of plays by women, and five of its marked successes in 1994 were by women. It has:

> ...a commitment to producing plays written by women and to ensuring that they are treated with the same respect as those written by men: i.e. that they are produced for both large and small venues and that they are considered equally for national and regional touring.

In looking back though their programs, they note that works by women dealt with a range of subjects and were equally produced by both the mainstream and TIE arms. Their executive manager states:

> I did note that scripts by women and new writers in general tended to play in the Cremorne Theatre, a venue significantly smaller than the Company's other hired venue, Suncorp Theatre.

La Boite's Artistic Director, Sue Rider states:

> Over the past three years, 50% of our plays have been by women writers. However, this proportion is becoming harder to maintain, due to the difficulty in finding suitable scripts.

Just Us indicates that it was started somewhat coincidentally by three women:

> ...with a view to creating performance that was not only entertaining but responsive to issues of community concern and social justice. Being in a regional location with a limited pool of actors, most of whom were female, tended to limit options ... and has led JUTE ... to producing its own work, written by female writers.

Kooemba Jdarra, a new company for indigenous artists, indicates:

> Due to a range of skills available in our community, Kooemba Jdarra finds a real reliance on women artists. As a young company we are

constantly addressing the need for training and opportunities for Murri artists to explore and voice their craft. The strength of women's stories and the individual strengths of women performers in our community has created a situation where the majority of our work (more than 3/4) has a woman's focus ... Two projects planned for 1995-6 will have all women cast and crew in acknowledgement of gender/cultural differences within Murri communities.

Rock'n'Roll Circus indicate that:

...most of our work is non-text based and therefore no writer is employed. There have been, however, 5 major exceptions, and of these major projects, 3 were written by women. Most of our directors, who play a strong conceptual role, have been women (12 out of 18).

Which works by women have been particularly notable?

At the Queensland Theatre Company two critically and financially successful productions were *Hotel Sorrento*, Hannie Rayson (1992) and *Diving For Pearls*, Kath Thomson (1993).

In 1993 *Composing Venus* by Elaine Acworth won the second annual George Landen Dann Award for playwrights. She is a local writer and at that stage was unproduced. Queensland Theatre Company opened their 1994 season with a production of this script:

Composing Venus is a remarkable first play ... Acworth's vision is a lyrical one, entwining public with personal histories, mythologising and rendering magical the gold boom town of Charters Towers from the 1920's to the night when Sputnik first sparked across the topical skies. Veronica Kelly, The Australian.

I suspect the drama of half a century's lost opportunities will have its strongest appeal for women, who may well identify with the ebb and flow of the lives suggested by MsAcworth's frequently poetic script. Des Partridge, The Courier Mail.

Jill Shearer has been very active in the Brisbane theatre scene for a number of years and last year the Queensland Theatre Company produced *The Family*. Dealing with corruption in the Queensland police force, it was set in the physical family of a father and son who were also members of the force. It will be shown at Sydney's Ensemble in 1996.

Street Arts mentions *Iyitha* by Therese Collie & Effie Detsimas as one of their most successful productions this year. Iyitha is a bilingual Greek/English script and was very popular with the Greek-Australian community.

Street Arts' *Through Murri Eyes* (1992) evolved from Maureen Watson's script concept. Director Kath Fisher, along with the cast and crew, improvised and collaboratively created the performance. Crucial to this development was the seeking of advice, research and feedback sessions with the Murri community in Brisbane. Sue Rider was the dramaturg.

Out of the Blue by Therese Collie dealt with women in prisons. It was produced in 1991 with Hilary Beaton as dramaturg and director.

Hilary Beaton is a very successful Brisbane writer and dramaturg. She has worked with most of the major companies currently in existence in Queensland and she actually earns her living through this work. She wrote *Trading Hours* for Street Arts and this was nominated for an AWGIE. The script looked at sexual harassment in the workplace. In 1990 Hilary's script, *No Strings Attached,* was included in the Playworks development program. Last year this script received its premiere production at La Boite Theatre.

> *Beaton has spent six years toiling through draft after draft to achieve her best shot. The result, with the creative input of the director, Sue Rider, is the best crafted new play by a Queensland writer in a long time and certainly the best among new plays by women this the year.* Sue Gough, Bulletin.

In the last two years, two of La Boite's productions of women's scripts have been selected for broadcast by ABC FM: *Painted Woman* by Sue Woolf and *She of The Electrolux* by Sara Hardy. Another hit for La Boite and Brisbane Rep was Mary Hutchison's *Did You Say Love*, also a huge hit at the Adelaide Fringe Festival.

Icy Tea is a community cultural organisation run by women. Over their eight years they have established a strong role within the Inala community. *"Through a variety of contemporary artforms we seek to inspire our communities in celebration of their voices."* All their performance works have been group devised and have toured extensively within the community as well as other venues around Brisbane.

Are women working in key creative roles?

Until recently the two major funded mainstream companies in Brisbane had women directors, Chris Johnson (QTC) and Sue Rider (La Boite). Chris has since resigned from the QTC. Other companies which are currently headed by women include: Just Us Theatre Ensemble, Icy Tea, Contact Youth Arts (co director), La Boite Youth Theatre and Twelfth Night Theatre.

In the early years this survey covers, women were not so prominent as directors.

In the administrative area women currently hold key roles in the following companies: La Boite Youth Arts, Renegade Theatre, Kooemba Jdarra, Rock 'n' Roll Circus, Contact Youth Theatre, Twelfth Night Theatre, Just Us Theatre Ensemble, Icy Tea, La Boite Theatre Company, Queensland Theatre Company and Street Arts. The two companies not included in this list, Snot Arts and The House Is Live! do not have a roles formally designated as administration.

From the companies that responded to this survey it is clear that women do hold major roles as directors, administrators, project coordinators and, in the case of youth theatre, tutors.

Only two companies have resident dramaturgs, QTC and La Boite. One of these positions is held by a woman, Louise Gough at La Boite Theatre. Other companies employ dramaturgs on a project by project basis. Hilary Beaton, for example, works as a dramaturg 'ear to ear' (telephone) with Just Us Theatre in Cairns. Josephine Fleming is the New Writing Coordinator at QTC.

What are the reasons given if there is a low proportion of women's work?

Although not at fifty percent, the proportion of work written by women is significant: to call it low is to underrate the achievements. Companies expressed support for the concept of new work by women writers.

Renegade Theatre is a company that formed this year to develop and produce new works by local writers. As yet they have not produced a play written by a woman. Next year they are scheduled to produce new works by Elaine Acworth and Fiona Munro. Clive Williams indicates:

As director of the Company I want to see Renegade produce plays by women writers. However, not as a politically correct act but rather to gain a different view of the world and its workings.

Gail Wiltshire of Twelfth Night Theatre:

I need two million dollars a year to sit in this venue, you cannot afford to take the risk on work you know can't sell.

Gail clearly thought that contemporary scripts and scripts written by women fell firmly into that category. Jean Pierre Voos, director of Tropic Line states:

I don't recall the Company expressing an opinion on the gender of the author.

He went on to explain that the Company responds to the quality of the script rather than who it was written by.

Ludmilla Doneman, co-Artistic Director of Contact Youth Theatre states:

The specific point of our work is not gender, but cultural background.

Cross cultural work embraces the work of many different groups, e.g. indigenous people. Within this work there is no special treatment for women. Both Contact and Snot Arts emphasised that they do not divide or prioritise their work along gender lines. Both organisations have women in key artistic and administrative positions.

What suggestions do companies offer to improve the situation?

There were only a few companies which felt that there was a situation that needed improving.

La Boite indicates that:

> *Sometimes women playwrights are selecting to express their work in complex forms, or else the content is itself complex. This can limit accessibility for an audience. On the other hand, plays like* Wallflowering *have immediate appeal and make excellent product for regional touring.*

Gail Wiltshire said that with funding she would definitely develop new works at Twelfth Night Theatre and would produce scripts written by women writers. Another strong commitment:

> *Renegade supports the beliefs of Playworks and we hope that you will consider our Company as a possible avenue for productions of plays that Playworks has helped develop.*

Kooemba Jdarra indicates:

> *In our brief history, Kooemba Jdarra has noticed that works written by women are better developed and contain more diverse and complex issues whereas male writers seem to have a dated perspective of the human condition and are overtly political in a didactic sense. Women embrace a collaborative approach to the development of new work yet maintain an integrity of purpose about the piece they are working on ... Anecdotal evidence shows that Murri audiences seem to connect more with female characters as a whole and especially within a dramatic world painted by female writers. Women writers deal with more contemporary human experiences and show a politic through the subtleties of the human face of a situation.*

from western australia

The Perth theatre community is currently living on shaky ground. Since the collapse of the state theatre companies and the movement of the WA Department for the Arts away from base funding and towards project funding the major companies are struggling between the balance of commercial success and producing new works and tending to go almost completely towards commercial success. It is basically assumed that a new work by an unknown woman can not be a commercial success. This is not only a problem with the way theatre companies think but with the way theatre audiences have been educated.

The belief that the numbers of women writing for theatre are low is more of perception than actuality. In my experience during playwrighting workshops and playwrighting laboratories there are equal if not more women participating so it then seems to be a problem of profile.

Sarah Brill

The Companies

Information was received from or about the following 14 companies:
Black Swan 1992-5; Hole-in-the-Wall; WA Theatre Company 1985-6; Barking Gekko 1988-1995; Hayman Theatre Co; Spare Parts; Theatre West 1993-1995; Yirra Yaakin 1993-5; Bizircus 1992-5; WA Actors' Centre 1991-5; State Theatre Co 1991-2; Perth Theatre Company 1988-95 (ex-SWY); Deck Chair Theatre.

There have been considerable changes in WA theatre over recent years, in particular in relation to the operation of the main state theatre company which has changed form in two crucial periods, from WA Theatre Company to State Theatre Company to Black Swan. The other theatres cover a range of community, classical, puppetry, circus youth and aboriginal theatre companies.

What proportion of work, over the past ten years, has been written by women?

Over the past ten years 30% of the total works performed in WA were written by women, of this number 27% were contemporary Australian writers. 70% of works were written by contemporary Australian writers (male and female), 28% of the works were directed by women. The total percentage of works dramaturged by women is only 4%, however this figure is not entirely accurate as in many cases records of dramaturges were not available and often dramaturgs (male or female) were not utilised.

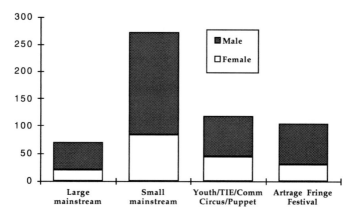

Figure 11: WA - Comparison of works written by women

Note: In place of the category Contemporary Performance, we have used the Artrage Fringe Festival statistics for this graph.

Black Swan Theatre Company indicate that they are as a main stage house aware of the importance of non discrimination. During their four years of operation, they have averaged 1 play out of 3 or 4 by a contemporary Australian woman writer. In the 1995 subscription season of 8 plays, however, mostly touring performances from, or in partnership with, other states, only *Diving for Pearls* was by a woman; an additional season of 6 short plays featured 2 women.

Deck Chair Theatre indicates that it:

> *...is committed to providing an environment in which women artists can produce work and a major part of the program is by, for and performed by women.*

Theatre West over its three years has concentrated on a play a year, mostly by women. The director Leith Taylor states, "I have always found it to be a nourishing and enriching experience to involve myself in other women's stories".

Yiraa Yaakin Youth Theatre is a training organisation set up to give Aboriginal theatre artists the skills to run a small community theatre company. Most plays are group devised but the overwhelming majority of members are female.

Barking Gecko Theatre Company (formerly Acting Out) is a young people's theatre group. It has been proactive in seeking work written by women and has averaged around 50% save for the past two years, when only one play written by a woman has been performed each year out of seven and five. Hayman Theatre Company is in fact a student organisation based at Curtin University. It concentrates on the classic repertoire and over the past ten years has had only one or two plays written by Australian women out of seven or eight productions of its major shows. They do, however, about 20 lunchtime shows a year, of which "30% would be written by women and 60% directed by women".

Performing Arts Centre Society is a theatre subsidy program similar to La Mama. Since April 1994, of 38 productions, 22 have been written and/or directed by women. The content of each is determined by the production group.

Which works by women have been particularly notable?

Sistergirl, produced by Black Swan Theatre Company and written by Sally Morgan was their second most successful production in the company's five year history. The Effie Crump Theatre Company state that their productions of *Lipstick Dreams* and *The Starting Stalls* have both run for successful seasons. *Emma,* devised by Emma Cicciolotto with Graham Pitts has been a great success and toured extensively. Mary Morris has won an AWGIE for *Too Far to Walk,* which was commissioned by Deck Chair. Deck Chair also commissioned *Barmaids* from Kath Thomson. In the past year, the co-devised performance piece, *Ningali*, by Ningali Lawford, has been an enormous success and has toured to the Edinburgh Festival and the Festival of Australia Theatre in Canberra.

Are women working in key creative roles?

Barking Gecko is one of the most proactive companies approached in regards to women. Although the position of artistic director is held by a man, their training artistic director is a woman as well as their set designer/production manager. Two past playwrights in residence have been women as well as five guest directors. Barking Gecko also advocates women for lead acting roles, which includes women playing lead male characters. Yirra Yaakin Youth Theatre Company employ a female director/workshop leader and a trainee company manager. Their membership is overwhelming female.

Leith Taylor worked for many years as a freelance director and actor. In the past three years she has been the sole artistic director of her own company, Theatre West.

Black Swan Theatre Company have no women in key creative roles; however they have recently employed a woman to the position of development and marketing, a role they hope will gain in importance. Black Swan Theatre Company also often work with Leith Taylor and her company Theatre West.

Because of its small size SWY Theatre Company existed for years with only one artistic director, a male. Due to financial constraints he directed all of their productions. As the Perth Theatre Company they now employ a female general manager.

Effie Crump Theatre Company's founder/artistic director is a women, as is their administrator. Spare Parts Puppet Theatre's associate artistic director is a woman and they employ female designers and performers. In Deck Chair Theatre Company the positions of artistic director and general manager within the company are held by women.

What are the reasons given if there is a low proportion of women's work? What suggestions do companies offer to improve the situation?

There seem to be two main responses to these particular questions. The first is a defensive one in which companies insist that works are chosen based on the quality of the work not on the gender of the writer. This then leads into the second response which is an apparent lack of women playwrights (for commissions) or scripts by women, so that in the choosing of a season of works, it is almost inevitable that the majority of the scripts will have been written by men.

Barking Gecko state that they need to seek out women writers. They felt that if this was not done then their program would be dominated by male writers. This is due to the fact that male writers continually approach the company with project proposals. They express a desire for women to be encouraged to approach their company with ideas and a desire to work with the company.

Yirra Yaakin Youth Theatre feel that young Aboriginal playwrights are scarce, particularly young women Aboriginal playwrights. However an overwhelming number of their members are female and it is through these members that pieces are collectively devised. On occasion members will express interest in writing a project of their own however there are not the staffing resources within the company to adequately develop this desire. In a move to improve this situation Yirra Yaakin is considering running playwriting workshops with more senior writers, such as Sally Morgan, and then following the workshops with a playwriting competition in the hope of providing incentive for young Aboriginal women.

Black Swan Theatre Company, who also have a specific interest in Aboriginal work, feel that women of Aboriginal descent need to be encouraged and nurtured towards writing for theatre. This thought is drawn from the success local publishing companies have had in producing prose written by local Aboriginal women. They also feel that there needs to be some incentive for theatre companies to undertake this nurturing process, before the script stage. Black Swan are also talking about creating a workshop area for their company where new works can be actively developed. They feel this will encourage an increase in the numbers of works developed by women playwrights.

Spare Parts Puppet Theatre feel the low proportion of women's work generally is

due to the lack of training opportunities in Australia for their specific area. Again nurturing of playwrights is brought up; however, it is in this company's specific interest that the art form be recognised in the national training institutions as a legitimate art form and a separate genre.

There also appeared to be an obligation felt by some theatre companies to produce classics. However for companies such as Hayman Theatre Company which is a university run company it is a requirement of the course. In the days of the state theatre companies this was also true and what are considered to be classics are almost always written by men.

Leith Taylor, director of Theatre West, states:

> *My personal experience is that women playwrights tend to be looser about their work, ready to change and adapt and less precious about keeping it intact. They also tend to have a great sense of humour which makes the collaboration enjoyable.*

Deck Chair indicate:

> *The company's work is strongly focused on commissioning new work and the production of premiere seasons and touring. Commitment is to new Australian work, women artists, non-dominant cultures and modern histories.*

from tasmania

Even though women fare extremely well here in Tasmania as far as key creative roles and even writing are concerned, Tasmania is viewed very much as a fringe state, and consequently there is not the prestige attached to these positions that there would be in some other states. For example, while Louise Permezel is the Artistic Director of a State Theatre Company, she also has to act as her own Administrator as the Company can't afford to employ a full time Administrator.

I am currently working on *Desires*, an adult puppetry show which will be produced later this year by Terrapin. The show involves five women playwrights, at various stages in their careers, and two of them living here in Tasmania. The agenda for this production was not to employ five female playwrights, that's just how it worked out, because the couple of male writers Annette Downs approached about the project said they wouldn't do it for the money she was offering! Annette Downs has commented, "men are less interested in writing for what they see as a fringe art form (puppetry), in a fringe city for fairly average payments". Five women, including myself, said yes to the project.

Terrapin have applied for funding from the Australia Council to promote the five writers involved in the project. As well, the production is touring to International Festival of Puppetry, in Budapest next year, and the National Script Centre, based here in Hobart, and run by a woman, is hoping to publish the scripts.

But on the whole female playwrights aren't doing too badly down this end of the country, and I think much of this is due to the fact that most of the theatre here is run by women. Perhaps the only thing hindering more work written by women being produced here is the conservative nature of the Tasmanian audiences.

Belinda Bradley

The Companies

The following 6 companies provided information:

Zootango; Theatre Now; Mummers Theatre; Rip and Tear; Terrapin Puppet Theatre; Salamanca Theatre Company.

No response was received from Gambit.

What proportion of works, over the past ten years, has been written by women?

With the exception of Zootango (The State Theatre Company), Rip and Tear Theatre (which to date has primarily devised work with members of the community and the two founding members of the Company), and Mummers Theatre (which mostly adapts traditional children's stories), all theatre companies (yes there are still others!) have had a high proportion of their work written or adapted by women over the past ten years, with the number steadily increasing in the last few years.

Zootango, while producing fewer plays per year, has slowly been increasing its work by female writers in the past couple of years, since the original Artistic Director and founder of the Company Richard Davey left, and Louise Permezel took over as Artistic Director.

Theatre Royal, the historic theatre in central Hobart has begun in recent years to act as a venue and to bring in plays, particularly through the Playing Australia scheme. Unfortunately it was not able to provide information to this survey.

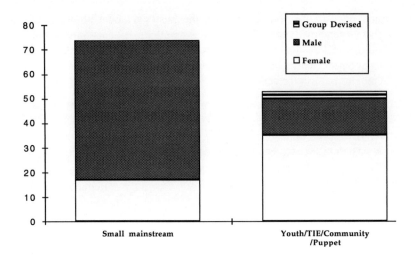

Figure 12: Tasmania - Comparison of works written by women

Which works by women have been particularly notable?

Highest Mountain, Fastest River, by Donna Abela, a play dealing with the Hmong community in Hobart, had two productions in separate years with Salamanca Theatre Company and won a Human Rights Award. Also successful was Noelle Janaczewska's *Marie Curie Chat Show*, a schools performance about women and science.

Wallflowering by Peta Murray had a long season; many people saw this production and enjoyed it. *Barmaids* by Katherine Thomson also had a successful and long season.

Are women working in key creative roles?

Ten years ago the majority of key creative roles in the funded companies were held by men. However, the last three to four years has seen a complete turnaround and now most of the key creative roles in the funded companies, particularly in the South of the state, are held by women.

Louise Permezel became the Artistic Director of Zootango late in 1993, (Zootango is the only 'mainstream' professional theatre company in Tasmania), and the other two major theatre companies, Terrapin Puppet Theatre and Salamanca (both touring schools), have female Artistic Directors, as well as a majority of women in key creative roles, as do Mummers Theatre and Gambit Theatre Company (both working with young people).

The 'mainstream theatre company to be' in the North of the state, Theatre North, has a female Administrator but women are outnumbered on the Management Committee and these are the people who make the decisions.

What are the reasons given if there is a low proportion of women's work?

Most of the Companies do not have a low proportion of work by women, with the exception being Zootango Theatre Company and Mummers Theatre, and with both of these companies there are signs of change for the better.

Mummers Theatre has to date mostly produced traditional work for children, most of which is not written by contemporary Australian writers, male or female. Things are gradually changing, and this year Mummers is using a female playwright for the first time. This has come about because the group financially responsible for the project (The Tasmanian Health Department) requested a female playwright, because of the issues involved, benzodiasepine addiction.

Companies are keen to use local playwrights, of which there are at least two male and two female living in the South of the state. Companies in the North of the state expressed a desire to work with local playwrights, male or female, but didn't know of any. Rip and Tear Theatre are working on a nation-wide project later this year and are interested in working with women on this project, either as writers or directors.

All companies commented that the quality of the work was the most important factor, and stressed that they were not for or against employing female writers, as long as they can come up with the goods!

What suggestions do companies offer to improve the situation?

Louise Permezel is currently supporting the development and work of three local playwrights, two male and one female, by acting as a dramaturg and providing access to actors employed by Zootango Theatre Company to workshop scripts. As well, Louise is bringing female writers into the state to write plays for the Company (Tobsha Learner) and to take workshops (Hilary Bell). Louise is hoping that the writing workshops, as well as helping established writers further develop skills, will also encourage new writers, male and female.

Terrapin are currently working with the two professional female playwrights living in Tasmania. Annette Downs, the Artistic Director, would like to encourage more people to write for puppetry, male or female.

Both Salamanca and Terrapin have a high percentage of work written, performed and directed by women. As the majority of their work is done in schools, they hope this will encourage young women to pursue any interest in theatre they may have. They hope their work will break down some of the stereotypes and barriers that are still rife in much of Tasmania, particularly in the north of the state which is generally more conservative.

Companies considered it important to support young writers, whether male or female and are keen to offer opportunities to young people interested in playwrighting to develop skills.

australian capital territory

The proportion of women's work performed in the ACT appears to be quite good, or at the worst, reasonable. Canberra has a small population, largely middle class, and, for all that it is conservative, it has been the nest for a determined feminist population. That is to say that in a city of Canberra's size and demography (small enough for networking and communication yet large enough not to be in each other's pockets; professional, educated and middle class) women can, and do, actively support women's work and men are drawn in also.

Fiona Navilly

The companies

Information was collected from 9 companies:

Canberra Youth Theatre; Company Skylark; Fortune Theatre (now defunct); Tango 160; Jigsaw Theatre Company; Women on a Shoestring; Eureka!;WBK; Splinters.

What proportion of work, over the past ten years, has been written by women?

According to accessible records of the companies responding to the survey, it seems that over the ten year period, 66% of the work presented has been written by women.

In theatre, Canberra has a history of independent groups producing original or non-mainstream work. Attempts to create a 'state theatre company' have collapsed. Over the past ten year period, Theatre ACT, under George Whaley's direction, disappeared to be replaced by Fortune, under the direction of Don Mamouney. This in turn disappeared, and groups emerging included Interact, a mix of mainstage and community theatre, which produced Jan Cornall's *Escape from a Better Place,* and Canberra Theatre Company, which between 1991 and

1993 was under the direction of Carol Woodrow. Woodrow indicates that she tried to do 50% Australian work and 50% women's writing as a commitment. Among the successes of this company were the premiere of Peta Murray's *Wallflowering*, which had large local audiences and went on to the Melbourne Spoleto Festival and Jennifer Paynter's *Balancing Act* picked up straight from a Playworks workshop. Paynter's rewriting of this as *Shackleton* went on to win ABC Radio awards.

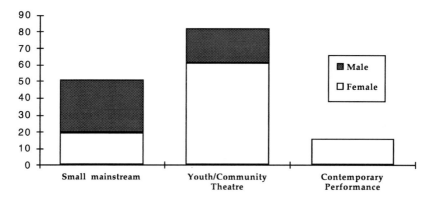

Figure 15: ACT - Comparison of works written by women

Woodrow has gone on to be involved in WBK an unusual combination of 3 theatre artists, Monica Barone, Boris Kelly and Carol Woodrow. They had great success with their first year in 1994, and *The Hyper-Real Thing*, developed and written by Barone and Kelly, was shown at Questacon, the National Institute of Science and Technology.

Audiences in general are still thin on the ground — or in the seats — except at the local Pro-Am company productions where the theatre is often full for 'tried and true' works, mostly written by men. National Festival of Australian Theatre dirrected by Robyn Archer has made over two years a very significant contribution, featuring women's writing.

However in the responses from the companies it can be seen that women's writing is dominant in the work of youth, community and puppetry companies. It seems that the committed audiences are open to seeing any work of value, irrespective of the gender of its author.

Canberra Youth Theatre suggests that:

> *This is somehow intrinsic to the nature of youth theatre — the process (workshop devising) appeals and is organic to women.*

Women on a Shoestring was specifically formed by director Camilla Blunden to address the unequal position of women in theatre. They have had some major successes in the past couple of years. *Empty Suitcases* written by Merrilee Moss was performed first in 1993, and over the past two years has been toured extensively through Playing Australia to NT, rural NSW, SA and Tasmania, with return ACT seasons. Another production with a long life has been *Over the Hill*, also by Moss, which has toured in 1995 to NT and the NSW Blue Mountains. *Child of the Hurricane,* by Moss and Mary Hutchison, is a play about Katherine Susannah Prichard, which has had considerable local success. Blunden suggests that there is a touring network which targets rural areas and where a number of works become great successes (in SA centres, they were described as the best show since Red Shed's *In Cahoots*), but which does not have any impact in the Sydney-Melbourne axis.

Since 1985, Splinters, a contemporary performance company working with words images, large puppets and music, has run as an artistic collective. They indicate:

> *Over a ten-year history, women performer-writers and dramaturgs have played a crucial role in all aspects of the shaping of the company's work.*

Most works are collectively written.

Are women working in key creative roles?

Women are working in key creative roles in Jigsaw Theatre, Women On A Shoestring, Tango One 60, which is a partnership between a man and a woman, People Next Door and Eureka!, where Camilla Blunden is now Artistic Director. Carol Woodrow continues as a free-lance director, as WBK did not receive funding from the ACT government in 1995, despite support from the Australia Council. Canberra Youth Theatre has had a long and proud history of women Artistic Directors and Associate Directors and, although that is not the case at present, there remains a strong and numerous presence of women amongst the tutor/directors who are also, by nature of the company, key creative personnel.

What suggestion do companies offer to improve the situation?

Eureka! produces contemporary Australian work. They point out that there are now a lot more plays by women:

> *Playworks has played a big role in that. Eureka! uses Playworks and finds it invaluable. It is crucial that women are in positions of decision-making when choosing scripts and not afraid to fight for women's writing 'cos men will present men's work that does not challenge their values.*

Fiona Navilly comments:

As an overall impression I can only add that women are quite well represented in ACT theatre in general and so there is a predisposition towards the performance of work of their own or by other women.

from northern territory

It's a small society. We can do things if we start them ourselves and are prepared not to have much money. Women have been very active in performing arts here.

Our major theatre company comments that when the company has looked for plays of quality, they have come predominantly from women in the last four years. That is positive news.

Suzanne Spunner

The Companies

This survey was based on information provided by the following 3 companies: Darwin Theatre Co; Corrugated Iron Youth Theatre; Salt, Fire Water.

Companies in Alice Springs are mainly amateur. The main venue is the Araluen Arts Centre.

What proportion of work in the past ten years has been by women? What can be done to improve situation?

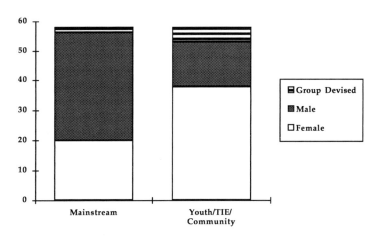

Figure 14: Northern Territory - Comparison of works written by women

Over the last decade there have only been two permanent funded companies in the Northern Territory and both are based in Darwin: Darwin Theatre Co (DTC), formerly Darwin Theatre Group, and Corrugated Iron Youth Theatre (CIYT).

Darwin Theatre Company has had a reasonable success in presenting plays by women and indeed has commissioned three women writers. This is considerable achievement in a situation of very low funding. Its statistics show a marked improvement in the proportion of women's work after 1987, when Mary Hickson was appointed artistic director. Since then women writers have averaged at 50% or better.

DTC had a strong tradition of playreadings which was abandoned for about five years and revived three years ago — approximately eight Australian plays are read and of these more than 50% are by women, including Hannie Rayson, Mary Morris, Joanna Murray-Smith and Hilary Beaton. 1995 featured classic Australian work following the ANPC series and included Dorothy Hewett and Dymphna Cusack.

Over the last two years seasons of new work by new local writers have been developed by DTC — all have been short one act pieces and of these half the writers have been women. Spunner is concerned that there appears to have been no real dramatugical work done on the plays.

While Corrugated Iron Youth Theatre invariably does new work, in the main its shows are created by the company as group devised pieces, are adaptations of shows created by other companies eg Sidetrack, Magpie etc, or are devised as movement based or to meet the needs of kids of differing abilities or with experts on e.g. landcare. The playwrights whose work has been done include Richard Tulloch and Keith Gallasch, in addition to the women writers in residence. Its statistics show a consistent representation of women's writing, but this must be analysed more.

A recent trend has seen the Artistic Director write the shows — this tends to arise as a result of limited funding and while the AD is a woman and the resultant pieces work as shows, they would not stand alone as scripts and Spunner suggests the company would benefit from being able to commission more often. Residencies have required a lot of extra work by the AD to look after and get the work from the writer, so it often seems and possibly is, more efficient to write the play.

In August 1993, Spunner co-ordinated the first NT Young Playwrights Weekend in conjunction with the ANPC and CIYT. Of four plays three were by Aboriginal youth of whom one was a girl from Alice Springs; all of them were brief and sketchy but valuable assertions of cultural identity. The fourth play was by a young woman from rural Darwin and it was the only play suggesting a promising writer. The second YPW is planned for later this year.

The State Theatre Company of the NT was a brief foray into theatrical grandstanding, which occurred in 1987. It was bankrolled by the NT government against the advice of the Australia Council but entirely dependent on funding being matched federally. After nine months and four productions it folded when the NT government money ran out. Of the four plays three were by Australian playwrights — all male. The Artistic Director, Peter Copeman and all the directors were men. The following year saw Copeman direct a Territory Rock Opera: *Come Hell or High Water* by Alice Springs writer Barney Foran which was produced by the Alice Springs Theatre Co (formerly Totem Theatre Group), an amateur group in Alice Springs. To summarise: in this entire venture there were no opportunities for women as writers/dramaturgs or directors.

Projects initiated by women theatre artists

Salt, Fire, Water, is a collective of women artists from English and non-English-speaking backgrounds. The present core group of five has multiple skills. The group began in 1994 with a group-devised show of three women's stories. A new group is now devising a sequel, *Breath of the Wind.*

WOW (women's own work) was a Darwin based women's theatre group formed in 1985 and over the next five years it staged a major production/short season annually. It was entirely self funded, and gave opportunities to women as directors. The first two shows were group devised cabaret performances, but in 1986, director Christine Boult invited Doreen Clarke to Darwin and she wrote *Ill Wind* for WOW which depicted the experiences of women and families during and after Cyclone Tracy. In 1987/8 four plays were produced - all were directed by Boult and Tessa Pauling. They comprised three works by English feminist playwrights - Louise Page, Micheline Wandor and Sarah Daniels, and John Romeril's *Mrs Thally F.* The group ran out of steam in 1988 but performer Aqua Robins and director Tessa Pauling joined forces with Suzanne Spunner to form Paradise Productions which subsequently workshopped and in some cases produced four works of Spunner's over the next five years — *Dragged Screaming to Paradise, Overcome by Chlorine, Magnetic North* and *Safe 'n' Sound.*

Important women performers/producers/writers include Bronwyn Calcutt, primarily a singer musician who writes her own cabaret style material; however she has branched out into writing a series of shows based on female spiritual and Jungian journeys such as *Women Of The Broken Circle*, a group devised work based on *The Wounded Woman*, which received Creative Development funding in 1991; *Disenchantment,* a one woman show which Bronwyn wrote/designed and performed, toured to Canberra and Adelaide; and *Skeleton Woman* — a large cast music theatre journey based on *The Women Who Run With The Wolves,* co-devised and co-directed with Rosalba Clemente, which received Creative

Development funding.

Betchay Mondragon is a Filipina who moved to Darwin in 1990. An experienced performer/director/deviser with PETA in the Phillipines, she has been active in a number of multicultural theatre events. Betchay has independently produced *Malache* by Virginia Jane Rose. In 1995 she has written/performed and co-directed the highly successful *Inday: Mail Order Bride*.

Alice Springs

There are very few playwrights in the centre but there are a couple of women who are keeping women's voice alive there. In general Centralian women tend to form mad cabaret groups e.g. *The Wendys*. Fiona McLoughlan is a stand up comic who has created her own shows and toured them around the NT in recent years. Mahoney Kiely put together independently a 1994 production *Baked Bean Dreaming* by Sydney writer, Jane Barton. It was a one woman show performed outdoors which Mahoney took to Katherine, Darwin and Adelaide.

Merrill Bray is an Arrente Aboriginal woman from the centre whose interest in writing about the stolen generation was kindled by Christine Dunstan, the former Director of Araluen Arts Centre. Peta Murray as writer in residence worked with Merrill on *Our Mob* staged in first draft form at Araluen in 1992 then at 1993 ANPC. Suzanne Spunner was appointed as dramaturg.

Which works by women have been particularly notable?

Among highlights have been:

1988 *Death At Balibo* - very successful and significant locally devised and written play about Timor, directed by Mary Hickson. The principal writer was Graeme Pitts with three Timorese writers including one woman, Maria Alice Casimiro (now a member of Salt, Fire, Water and LAFAEK, the NT Timorese Cultural Group).

1990 *The Ingkata's Wife,* by Suzanne Spunner, was staged in Alice Springs and Darwin. The project was directed by Janet Robertson, developed for and with Jenny Vuletic; it was about Kathleen Strehlow, the widow and second wife of Ted Strehlow. An epic drama about Cultural ownership.

1991 *Wallflowering* - Peta Murray's play was selected as the first play DTC would put on in the 700 seat Playhouse at Darwin Performing Arts Centre. It was significant that a play by a contemporary woman writer was regarded as the most likely to be commercially viable in this venue — it went well.

1992 *Barmaids,* by Katharine Thomson, an extremely successful local production had a sell out season then toured to Alice Springs and down the track.

1993 *Heartbeat* was put together for The Indigenous Youth Conference by The Mills Sisters — three Aboriginal women from Darwin who are singer/ performers; the show was very successful and toured the Top End and Kimberley aboriginal communities.

1994 *Dragged Screaming To Paradise* (Spunner) had already toured the Territory and was chosen for the programme as the play to open the 300 seat Studio Theatre; it proved to be the most successful DTC production ever, and later toured to Melbourne for The International Festival.

Are there women in key creative roles?

Over the period DTC has had 5 Artistic Directors (ADs) and one was a woman, Mary Hickson. The administrators have numbered 7 in that period and one, Stuart Gunning, was not female. Meanwhile CIYT has 5 ADs including one male, Stephen Gration, and all their administrative assistants have been female.

Writing residencies - Allyson Mills is currently Aboriginal Artist in Residence (with some writing component, though essentially she is a singer musician/ performer and occasional songwriter) with DTC but over the decade all the Writers in Residence have been male playwrights.

CIYT has had three writers in residence — Rosemary Fitgerald, Suzanne Spunner, Eva Johnson in 1993. They have never commissioned a male playwright.

Once Upon a Time

Once upon a time, a female researcher interviewed a male artistic director of a major theatre company. She was interested in why the company produced no works by women writers, and had not, for the past many years.

"How do you explain the imbalance?" she asked.

"I can't," he replied, although he hastily added that he didn't think it had anything to do with sex, meaning gender.

"Yes, there are lots of men in key decision making positions but at least we're all straight."

"I'm sorry?" she thought he meant conservative.

"I mean we're not a gay mafia."

He went on to explain his impressions of the unsolicited scripts they received.

"I don't think there is a difference in terms of quality between male and female writers. Nor in aesthetic, nor in numbers of scripts received", he said. And yet he expressed surprise that an "intelligent, hard-hitting script on political corruption" had turned out to be by a woman in the suburbs. He wouldn't have been surprised it she had written a fluffy romance. Interestingly, she had put only her initials on the script rather than a name.

"When it comes down to play selection," he said, "it's about quality and not taking financial risks".

"But I don't think it has anything to do with their genitals," he said. The researcher sighed, knowing he again meant gender. At least he got the first three letters right.

It must have been another country. Wouldn't happen here...

The State of Play

In summary, the statistics, such as they are, show that there is in most states a ·rather similar proportion of work written by contemporary Australian women in the programming of companies. In the smaller states and territories, where there is greater merging between professional and amateur traditions, women writers (and indeed directors) are likely to play a significant role.

The more detailed statistics show that in those fields where work is group-devised or experimental, there is equality of opportunity between male and female creators. Particularly in NSW where a number of companies define themselves as performance companies, or as experimental or physical companies, there are companies where partnerships, often of male and female performers, develop and devise work on the basis of equal commitment.

Women writers in all states feature strongly in the programming and development of work by community theatre companies, theatre for young people, and puppetry companies. All these fields consistently develop new work, and thus offer opportunities both for emerging and experienced writers.

The area where there is greatest imbalance is in the more traditional mainstage companies. Smaller companies, regional companies and state companies in smaller states do not often reach more than 25% of works by contemporary Australian women writers. It is difficult to draw any comparability between states in this matter, as complete figures were not always available. However, it would seem that in smaller states and territories the mainstage companies will feature work from women writers and have often had marked successes, for example with *Wallflowering* and *Diving for Pearls*. In NSW where there is a network of regional theatre companies performing mainstream works, the situation however is uneven.

Most interestingly, in the companies where there is the largest investment of resources, and which play to the largest houses, the four large State Theatre Companies, Playbox and Black Swan, which have now been brought by the Australia Council into the Major Organisations Board (MOB), women writers are poorly represented. Figure 15 shows that in fact the situation has not changed over the ten years of this study.

This is the only ten-year picture of a comparable group we could produce, because figures were not always available. Even here, major organisations or producers of Australian work would have been slightly different in 1985 than in 1995. Black Swan has been in existence for only five years, and so we have drawn figures from the WA Theatre Company. With all these provisos, it still seemed useful to consider the subscription programming of these six companies over a ten year period.

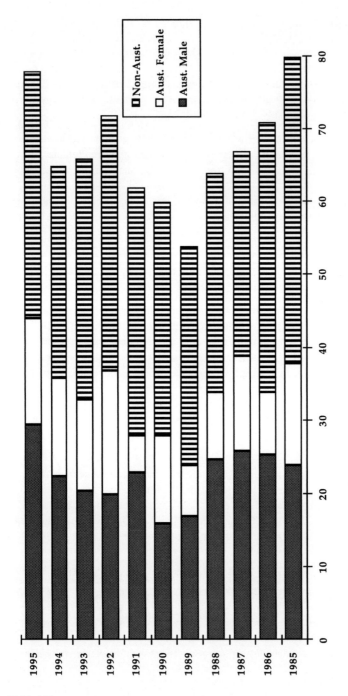

Figure 15: Major performing arts organisations programming 1985 - 1995

Numbers of plays performed

What Figure 15 shows is that in 1985, these six companies produced 80 plays in their major seasons; 14 of these were written by contemporary Australian women writers, and 24 by contemporary Australian male writers, with 42 from classical, international or non Australian repertoire. In 1995, they produced 78; of these 14.5 were by Australian women, 29.5 by Australian men, and 34 from other sources. The latter figure is high considering that Playbox (and to some extent, Black Swan), is dedicated to only Australian work. In other words, over the ten years, we have begun to see a greater focus on contemporary Australian work, but this has not benefited women writers, whose work has hovered just under 20% of the seasons, although it dropped in one year to only 8%. Australian men's works have risen from 30% of the repertoire to 38%. From the company responses it also seems that women are more often consigned to smaller theatres or to seasons of one-act or short plays.

That's it for the figures. As we have suggested earlier in this report, measuring proportions of women's work is only useful at a very simplistic level. We have analysed the figures for this particular group of companies only in order to see if the perception by women writers that their work is infrequently performed by mainstream theatres is an accurate one. The figures that have been drawn together suggest that it is.

Most of the larger companies indicate the obstacles they see to works by women being performed. They are operating at a high level of investment and are increasingly reliant on box-office and corporate support as the proportion of government money declines. This has a marked effect on their programming decisions. They feel they must program conservatively, balance risks against successes. Some argue that the need for finding works which will be a guaranteed success and cover costs has led them to program noted successes from Broadway and the West End. Most argue they have a charter and responsibility to present work from the classical canon. They also argue they need to program big plays, plays dealing with the public world, major ideas and theories; this is accompanied by the supposition that women do not write such plays.

The Playworks survey does show that all companies think seriously about the issues of developing new Australian work, and work by women writers. There is an awareness of their responsibilities to encourage the building up of an Australian repertoire. The companies responding to our survey present a number of ideas to develop a performing arts culture and industry in which women played a significant part, and these we consider in the next section.

f i v e

Proposals for the future

The question with which Playworks embarked on this research was:

How can Playworks (and others like us) further improve the position of Australian women writers for performance?

We have canvassed writers, performing arts companies, funding agencies and development bodies.

This Playworks survey of women writers and performing arts companies demonstrates that the ten years between 1985 and 1995 have made an enormous difference to women writing for theatre and performance in Australia. When Playworks began in 1985 there was a sense of frustration among women writers. This frustration was shared by women as directors, who wanted to find plays with which they could identify, and by women actors, many of whom believed that women writers would provide them with roles which were more related to their experience.

Our proposals in this section highlight the complex process which makes up the production of performing arts in Australia. Individuals, funding bodies, development agencies and companies are aware of the issue and have presented a range of suggestions as to how Playworks can fulfil its aims of assisting women writers for performance to get their best quality work presented to audiences. These proposals go beyond the mere insistence on equity in numbers. Instead we aim to ensure that there are changes within the performing arts overall to ensure that good quality works are reaching audiences which actively want to see them.

The views of women writers

Australian writing has immeasurably transformed our theatre since the 1970s. Since the mid-1980s, women writers for performance have added their contributions in significant numbers, particularly influencing youth, community and experimental performance areas. Others have made major contributions to the canon of Australian works on mainstages, providing a mirror in which audiences can consider their own society.

Women writers are aware of and welcome their increased opportunities. There is a feeling of excitement among many respondents who see themselves as having a unique perspective and the skills to present it.

In particular, writers for the experimental,community and youth theatre value the seemingly boundless opportunity of being free of established definitions, to bring to audiences vibrant Australian voices, to create new writings for performance. These are the voices of the new Australian theatre. Yet there are also concerns expressed that these areas are denied resources, incomes, prestige and informed critical response, frequently dismissed to a 'margin'.

Many women suggest that the canon of work in theatre that our culture reveres, publishes, studies, continues to be male dominated; most directors of major companies are men. But many writers are eager to ensure that the new visions advanced by women, in the new forms which they are able to present them will alter this situation.

Some respondents believe that their work has been subject to a male judgement about the relevance of its content, theme, form and dramatic impact, particularly if they write from a feminist perspective.

Action to press for equal representation of women as managers, directors, playwrights, while helping greatly, may not make quick changes to deep-seated, centuries-old attitudes of men (and some women) that women's stories do not make good theatre. It is important that women writers take heart from the succeses written by women that have recently featured in the programs of major companies.

Many writers suggest that women are disadvantaged because of their responsibilities for home and family. It is not only the time taken by these responsibilities, but also the constraints that they place on women's ability to network in theatres and develop ongoing collaborative relationships.

A number made proposals which related to the structure of performing arts as a whole. Since many of these relate to play development, they are dealt with later in this section.

Focusing on Writers

The long term prognosis seems to be positive. Women have gained insights into their writing. They are determined to write so well that their work will survive any misinterpretation. They draw confidence from the fact that well over half of the audience is female. They anticipate that this will increase a demand for women writers. Encouraged by the positive changes that have taken place and whatever the obstacles, most of the women responding show a determination to continue to express their point of view and to do it through their writing.

Writers will always write. Yet in performing arts, with its needs for strong collaboration to get works performed, encouragement is necessary. The consistent attention provided to writers by development organisations and performing arts companies is important in ensuring that work reaches its best.

Getting the work before an audience is a further step. Among writers in our survey there are those who might be regarded as self-motivators with good track records and yet these writers have the same difficulties as less experienced writers in getting through the barriers of artistic directors with their eyes on the low risk subscription season. These writers need workshops in how to talk about their work, self-management, employment options, role models, more sophisticated forms of dramaturgy and strategies to develop collaborative relationship with agents and companies. Playworks can help to provide these.

Other respondents are less experienced and have difficulty promoting their own work or being taken up by agents. For these writers who lack any form of advocacy, Playworks acts in a necessarily limited way as a broker between writer and agents/companies/sources of production.

Assistance and funding for women writers

Since 1984, the Australia Council, as the major funding body for the arts, has responded to equal opportunity legislation and instituted programs to assist women against any discrimination. The analysis in this survey shows that over the past ten years the Australia Council and other government funding bodies have implemented measures through which women can achieve a comparable standing to that of men. The Australia Council has ensured that women are aware of the importance of funding possibilities and that they apply for grants. Our research shows that the Australia Council over the period has directed an equal or relatively equal proportion of grants in writing for performance categories to women writers. Although there are occasional inconsistencies, women are obviously gaining significant assistance to practice their craft.

The opportunities that government funding offers to develop practice, to travel for experience and research and to take time to concentrate on writing are all beneficial. But it is also important to ask whether merely increasing the amount of funding available for commissions and writers' projects is really the most effective way of ensuring that more work by women is performed.

The answer is that it is certainly important but only part of the story. The statistics on work performed indicate that commissions are not always carried through to production. We need to do more to get works from development stage into public performance.

The Australia Council has taken account of women's domestic responsibility in its decisions about grants and acknowledges that inability to afford childcare is another factor in women's disadvantage. Childcare is now an agreed component of grants. Nonetheless its provision is assumed to free women to follow traditional paths of self-fulfilment, to take up travel grants and research fellowships. These assumptions are still based on a male career path and may not suit women who need more flexible arrangements. Women writers with domestic and child care responsibilities may find difficulties with the long hours and informal collaborations which are such a vital part of performing arts culture.

The Australia Council has also assisted women writers, and indeed all other writers, by funding development organisations such as the Australian National Playwrights Centre and Playworks, the latter specifically to work with women. ANPC statistics show that the proportion of work by women developed and workshopped at their conference has increased substantially. A number of women writers expressed concern at the one-off showcasing of plays employed in traditional training institutions and national conferences. Playworks has worked on longer-term development of works, and ANPC and others are also working in this way.

In short, a consideration of the statistics for support and development of writers for performance suggests that women writers have benefited from determined efforts within funding bodies to improve equity.

Improving the Funding and Assistance Context

Playworks supports the Equal Opportunity model. It has achieved a lot. It has raised consciousness of the possibility of women's contribution to Australian theatre culture but our survey shows there is still a long way to go to ensure true equity. *The age of Equal Opportunity is not over.*

Similarly, suggestions that Australia has more than enough artists and now is the time to 'narrow the gate' prevent us taking full advantage of the carefully developed programs up to now. These programs and company policies have opened the door. *Now is not the time to close it.*

Furthermore, the current funding model does not question whether the categories under which grants are offered are always appropriate for women's interests and work patterns. Individual grants targeted at 'professionals' fail to take account of the working patterns which domestic and family responsibilities demand. There are strong indications that women may begin to write after other periods of work. This may mean that they take longer to develop reputations as writers than men of an equivalent age. This has major implications in the light of Australia Council draft proposals to award fellowships only once and to give greater preference to younger artists.

Playworks therefore encourages the Australia Council and other funding bodies to continue to monitor policies so that all Australians have equal access to the possibilities of expression afforded by the performing arts. Affirmative action for women has been an important spur to enriching our theatrical culture. The encouragement of writers from all areas of our multi-cultural society is also important. Playworks works to shift notions of margin and centre, to fight for equity for all writers and consequently for a truly representative theatre culture. In 1996 our major project takes account of this by focusing on writers from non-English speaking backgrounds.

Performing arts companies discuss the production of work by women

Playworks' state by state survey documents the programming of performing arts companies over the past ten years. There have certainly been signs of improvement in the number of productions of works by women writers. There has been an increase in the number of performance companies producing new and innovative work. Women are well represented in these companies, collaborating, devising, working across artistic forms. Women writers contribute a considerable body of work to theatre for young people and community-based companies and project.

Production numbers are still low proportionally in large mainstage companies. There are some active development programs by State companies but women are often concentrated as part-time dramaturgs and assistant directors, their work more often shown in brief seasons of Shorts and New Works, and in smaller venues.

These companies state that they have a charter and responsibility to present work from the classical canon and the international repertoire. Such policies will limit the proportion of work by women. Since historically women have not written for the stage, these companies will always present more work by male playwrights from the classical repertoire. There is a limit to the number of times Aphra Behn can be performed! Internationally, Wendy Wasserstein is one of the few women represented regularly on Broadway, just as Caryl Churchill is in London.

It is more worrying to read some of the responses about the programming of new Australian works. Companies argue that they must program conservatively, balance risks against successes. Some companies state that they need to program big plays, plays dealing with the public world, major ideas and theories; this is accompanied by the supposition that women do not write such plays. Any consideration of recent Australian successes would put paid to this perception. David Williamson's recent plays, which have been enormously successful for state theatre companies, are, in essence, domestic comedies of manners, about families, sexual harassment, the fallibility of friendship. Yet women writers have recently had produced plays about police corruption (Jill Shearer), industrial restructuring (Katherine Thomson) and other issues which are major issues and of political importance. It is stereotyping to assume that certain subjects are the preserve of one gender and stereotyping to assume that only certain subjects are of 'major significance' to audiences. The fact that audiences are still predominately female is surely another consideration here.

The findings of the survey cast questions over the often-repeated assertion that women artistic directors and directors often advance the careers of women writers. While this is demonstrably true in some cases, in others it hasn't happened. Women artistic directors operate under the same financial constraints as male artistic directors. Female directors equally search out works of quality, works which have a spark, make them excited; these can be by women or men. The operation of these decisions is a matter of timing chance, finances ... and chemistry.

The survey is also useful in providing evidence of how regionalised Australia's performing arts industry continues to be. While some plays are toured and become nationally known and popular, some may only be shown once in the state where they were developed. This is a matter of concern, considering both the development that has gone into those plays or performances and the lessons that can be derived from a first production. The development of a national touring network should assist this process, and the growth of venues for performance such as the National Festival of Australian Theatre in Canberra. Playing Australia should do more to encourage touring networks which cross boundaries, so that a range of good new work from the regions and smaller states in all genres is seen in major centres.

Working with Performing Arts Companies

Far from being just about equal numbers, there are important steps to be taken within the culture of performing arts companies to ensure the best work by women writers is presented as it should be.

Some of our respondents feel that conventional theatre companies and practices are resistant to change. Many of them are succeeding in new areas of writing (experimental performance, radio writing, multi-media). Our survey points to Contemporary Performance as an area of equal representation. Playworks acknowledges this as a place in which many women write, perform and self-produce. We, therefore, along with many of our respondents and experimental performance companies, welcome the creation of the Hybrid Arts Committee as recognising the importance of challenging the very structures of the theatre, the relationship between artforms (physical theatre, dance-theatre, music-theatre, multi-media performance), between audience and performer. In these freed spaces it seems women writers are allowed much broader scope for their ideas. Each year, more and more Performance works are taken into the

Playworks program. We need to adapt our developmental programs to take account of these new ideas and build on our already fruitful collaborations with Contemporary Performance Spaces throughout the country.

Writing for community and youth theatre are similarly fertile sites for new languages, new work by women writers. Yet this is another marginalised, under-resourced sector, where funding has been reduced and companies have disappeared, particularly in Victoria. These areas remain essential sources for developing new and wider audiences for performing arts. There must be more encouragement to companies to look at the possibility of cross-over between these areas and mainstream theatre, a route taken by some recent successes.

There are signs in our survey that some major organisations are taking more account of women writers, but improvements in equal representation are still small. Playworks is therefore concerned that large scale devolution of funds to the Major Organisations Board with reduced programming accountability may make the situation for women writers worse. *Will there be a place for women writers in these companies if they are not obliged to consider them?*

These companies argue they have a responsibility to reflect a canon of major works. It is important to ensure that when they are presenting works from an Australian repertoire that attention is paid to women writers whose work may have been neglected. The Australian National Playwrights Centre has shown that works by writers such as Cusack, Pritchard, Brand, Roland and Gray still speak to Australian audiences

There is evidence that these companies have a cultural conviction that plays by women are not major works, are too risky to produce and do not please audiences. It must be pointed out that none provided any real evidence of these assertions. It is nowhere proved that new plays by Australian women are likely to be a greater risk than new plays by Australian men, if they have been adequately developed and resourced. Indeed our surveys show that plays by Peta Murray and Katherine Thomson have opened major houses in smaller states, and that in SA, the State Theatre Company had high subscription numbers during a period when a number of plays by women were in the repertoire. What the survey suggests is that the major organisations produce plays by a relatively small number of well-known and experienced male dramatists. For women playwrights, with less experience and audience recognition, getting plays accepted is hard, just as it is for emerging male dramatists. It is important that these companies continue to focus on development programs and productions for new writers. Playworks is eager to assist with this process.

There is disturbing evidence that women do not submit plays to the major companies for consideration, not surprising given that a number of the companies do not demonstrate that they have selected from open submissions. It is important to ensure that there is selection from open submissions and that women writers' work is available for consideration during selection times. Playworks will follow up suggestions from several companies for future joint projects and cooperative work, to ensure that women writers are better integrated into the culture of major companies.

Developing the Audience

Responses from both writers and companies indicates how under-developed audience research is in the performing arts in Australia. Writers report on enthusiastic audience responses, but have no sense of numbers. Companies report on reactions by some subscribers or audience members, but there is little sense of audience response being systematically researched. Should there be more intensive market research to assess the appropriateness of all overseas successes for Australian audiences? Further questions relate to how much audience reactions relate to people's own prejudices, how tastes can be developed, how marketing can be expanded. Playworks is interested in exploring ways we might assist audience development by relying not on perceived taste but by establishing a dialogue between audience and companies. Playworks will consider ways to showcase work in development, to establish audience demand for writers' work and engage subscription audiences in a dialogue with new work.

The role of development agencies

Women speak of development, networking and collaboration as vital to their lives as writers. They value groups such as Playworks which put them in touch with other writers and directors. The female writer is offered far fewer mentors and role models than the male writer whose work has been more often performed and studied.

Other perceptions relate to the importance of networking. Theatre is a collaborative medium and familiarity with writers and their work is important for directors, designers and all creative personnel. Women and their representative groups have an important role here.

The commitment of significant time to development of new works is also another important step to be taken. It is now understood that ongoing development, sustained over a long term, is crucial for this to work. The links between companies and development organisations such as the Australian National Playwrights' Centre and Playworks will be vital for this process.

Some women speak of a fragile sense of self-esteem and setbacks that stop them writing for many years. Playworks will explore strategies to assist in confidence building

Australia has a growing tertiary training sector and work here, with women students and trainers, is important. The growth of new technologies is also significant in the development and promotion of women's writing and we need to ensure that women writers have easy access to these technologies.

Expanding the role of development agencies

The survey makes it clear how important the role of development agencies like ANPC, Playworks and writers' centres are to isolated writers. Organisations like ours provide ways in which individuals and groups can interact, receive information, maintain contact with producers, monitor market developments, promote and distribute work nationally and internationally and gain access to new training and professional development. We need to develop better strategies to cover the country, reach out to isolated groups, effectively and equitably disperse information and support.

New writers need help in relating to dramaturgs, directors, actors, designers and to hearing their work. Playworks 1996 Workshop Program takes account of some of these needs (Reading Room, Acting for Writers, Visualising Text, Writing for Space). Writers also need to develop skills in time management and motivation. They also need to know how to correspond with companies and to talk to agents.

At the same time, Playworks can continue to materially influence the take up of women's work by lobbying, working with companies, creating databases, directories, making referrals, encouraging strategic alliances, speaking to the press, providing workshops and improving the training of writers and dramaturgs.

Women's writing for performance is emerging as a significant force in Australia's performing arts. The past ten years have seen enormous growth in the production of works by women writers. The future looks promising, particularly considering the increased numbers of women writing for performance.

We will hear their voices

It's just a matter of time.

endnotes

1   Australia Council, *Public Attitudes to the Arts,* 1990, p, 3; Australian Bureau of Statistics, *Attendance at Selected Cultural Venues,* 1992, p12; Hull, A., 'Programs for Women Artists', *Refractory Girl,* 37, 1990, p 9.

2. Department of Employment, Education and Training, *Gender Equity and the Arts,* Draft Report, 1992.

3. Throsby, D. and Thompson, D., *But What do You Do for a Living?* Australia Council, 1994.

4. Women and Arts Research Group, *Women in the Arts,* Australia Council, 1983.

5. Throsby, D. and Thompson, D., *But What do You Do for a Living?,* Australia Council, 1994; Throsby, D. and Mills, D., *When Are You Going to get a Real Job?* Australia Council, 1989.

6. Heiler, R., *Childcare Needs of Non-Performing Artists,* 1991; Guldberg, G., *The Australian Music Industry,* 1987; Crouch, M. and Lovric, R., *Gender as a Theme in Professional Music Careers,* 1990; Prosser, C., *Visual and Craft Artists,* 1989. All Australia Council.

7. Rogers, V., Baldock, C. and Mulligan, D., *What Difference Does It Make?* Australia Council and WA Department for the Arts, 1993, passim and pp 93-97.

8. Swanson, G., Institute for Cultural Policy Studies and Wise, P., Australian Institute for Women's Research and Policy, Griffith University, *Women's Participation in the Arts and Cultural Industries in Queensland,* Australia Council and Arts Queensland, 1995. This publication has not yet been published and its recommendations are confidential. Playworks is grateful to the two funding Departments for permission to quote findings from the survey of artists which are relevant to our questionnaires.

9. Cox, E. and Laura, S., *What Do I Wear in a Hurricane?* Women in Film and Television, 1992, pp 26-30, p45.

10. *Glasgow Herald,* 29 July, 1986.

11. Crimeen, B., *Sunday Herald-Sun,* Melbourne, 2 May, 1991.

12. Tait, P., *Converging Realities: Feminism in Australian Theatre,* Currency Press/ Artmoves, Melbourne, 1994, pp 86-7.

13. Tait, P., *op. cit.,* p. 159.

appendix 1
how playworks conducted the survey

Playworks applied for a grant from the then NSW Ministry for the Status and Advancement of Women in January 1995. Responses were delayed by the NSW elections and the change of administration to the Department of Women.

We designed the questionnaire and trialled it among writers and performing arts companies. Their enthusiastic response led to a further request to the Australia Council Strategy and Communications Branch to provide funding to extend the research to the rest of Australia.

Notification that both grants were successful was received in June. Funding was devoted to employing researchers to analyse the results and to follow up writers and performing arts companies who had not responded,

Mailing lists for women writers were collected from the organisers of the Third International Women Playwrights' Conference, Playworks' own mailing list, the Australian National Playwrights' Centre, Writers' Centres and agents. Over 240 surveys were sent out. When these were followed up by telephone a number of women indicated that they were no longer writing, or specialised only in screen writing, and were not therefore appropriate respondents. When account is taken of the number of writers who had changed address, gone overseas or like Robyn Archer were organising two conferences, and had no time to respond, our final numbers of 90 are quite reasonable.

In addition surveys were sent to 113 performing arts companies funded by the Australia Council in 1994-5. These were then added to at state level by a search of Arts Ministry files, to pick up companies funded by the state or companies which had ceased operation during the past ten years. Data on these was sought by a search of arts ministry files. Within the constraints imposed by our time limit, so that we could publish for Playworks Tenth Anniversary Festival, 13-15 October, 1995, the final tally of 111 companies provides a good cross-section.

Playworks in the 6 weeks devoted to finalising the report has not had the time or resources to analyse all the data provided. We are happy to keep the data and use it for further analysis if resources are available and would appreciate any proposals from other researchers. We would also welcome any corrections to information in this book, as we have been often reliant on people's memories and interpretations.

A note of concern must be expressed about data. The state-based researchers found it extremely difficult to find reliable sources for data and records. Some companies have ceased existence and their complete records have not been placed in archives or in arts funding bodies' files. Other small organisations do not have the resources to maintain archives on their subscription series, brochures and programs. In the Australia Council, files for companies include both confidential information such as grant applications and publicly available information such as programs and annual reports. Previous years are now lodged in the Commonwealth archives and are expensive to access. In many states, archives charge high prices for research. It would seem desirable that an agreed base-line of material on each company (subscription brochures, programs, annual reports etc.) be deposited in a free and publicly accessible collection to ensure that there is easy access to our recent history.

appendix 2
women writers featured in this survey

The following list gives brief information on the writing histories of the women writers in our survey. Those writers marked with an asterisk (*) have been part of Playworks development program over the past ten years. More detailed information on these writers can be found in the second edition of the Playworks Directory, which gives full information on the works developed and their performance history.

Paula Abood
Has developed a collaborative choreo-poem *The Politics of Bellydancing* which has been performed in Sydney and Canberra by The Arab Feminist Alliance.

Lois Achimovich
Meekatharra was produced by Black Swan Theatre Company at the Playhouse in Perth in 1993. *John Boyce O'Reilly*, a group developed community play, was commissioned and produced by Deckchair Theatre. *Sukarno* has been developed and workshopped with Playworks and the WA Theatre Company.

Elaine Acworth
Elaine wrote her first play, *Torched*, in 1990. *Composing Venus* was produced by QTC in 1994. *Solitary Animals* will be staged by STC in 1996. She is currently working on *BOD* and *The Last Known Day of the Queen of the Night*.

Melle Amade
A performance piece, *Into the Heart,* has been staged at Sydney's Performance Space. Plays include *Cage, The Butterfly Spirits are Purring* and *Eros Sleeps with Psyche* .

Linda Aronson*
Linda Aronson writes for theatre and film. Two plays, *Dinkum Assorted* and *A Night with Robinson Crusoe* were workshopped and showcased by Playworks. *Dinkum Assorted* published by Currency Press, was an HSC text and has had many productions. *Reginka's Lesson* has been produced by Playbox.

Virginia Baxter*
Virginia Baxter is the co-writer and co-producer of collaborative performance works for theatre, galleries and radio produced by Open City, the company she formed with Keith Gallasch in 1987. Works include *The Girl With a Stone in Her Shoe, All That Flows, The Museum of Accidents, Tokyo Two, Sum of the Sudden, Sense* and *Shop & The Necessary Orgy*. Virginia is currently working on a CD-ROM performance project on the subject of Australian Englishes.

Hilary Beaton*
Hilary's plays include *No Strings Attached, Sitting on a Fortune* and *Outside In*. Works commissioned by TIE and/or community theatre companies include: *Worlds Apart,On the Line, Taken for Granted, Trading Hours* and *Giving Up the Ghost*. Hilary has received a Matilda Award from Queensland critics and her work has been published by Playlab Press.

Hilary Bell*
Hilary's plays include *Conversations with Jesus* and *Fortune* , which was produced by Griffin Theatre. Her radio plays have been produced by ABC Radio and she has written several short films. Hilary wrote the lyrics for Belvoir St.'s *Cockroach Opera* and her musical *The Wedding Song* was presented by the NIDA Company in 1994. *Fortune* is published by Currency Press.

Jennifer Bethel
Jennifer is currently working on a new play, *Seers,* following *Relinquishing* (1987).

Sue Bonaretti
A new writer whose first work is a musical play, *Lipstick.*

Barbara Bossert Ramsay
Barbara has written for the stage and for TV. Her plays include *The Accidental Mystic*, which was performed in Sydney, Melbourne and at the Edinburgh Festival and musical theatre works *Kiss Me Goodnight Sgt. Major, Hollywood Canteen of 1945* and *The Fabulous Rise of the Rhythm Sisters and The Method Brothers*

Belinda Bradley*
Belinda has written five plays, co-written and directed another, and adapted two for production on ABC Radio National. In 1991 there were productions of her plays, *The Killing of Grandma* and *The Other Woman. No Time to Play* was given a workshop and showcase reading by Playworks in 1990. Her short piece for puppets, *Mary*

May, is being produced in late 1995 at Terrapin Puppet Theatre. *Ordinary Lives* will be performed at La Mama Theatre in October 1995.

Anna Broinowski
Anna Broinowski is a writer, director and actor. Her first play, *The Gap*, (published by Currency Press), was performed at Belvoir St. Theatre in 1993 as part of the Sydney Asian Theatre Season. It has subsequently been performed in Canberra at the National Festival of Australian Theatre and has toured to Japan. Work for film includes *Bondi No Nami*, and *Hell Bento!!*

Anne Brookman
Anne Brookman has written extensively for the stage, including many works for children and young people such as *The Yinga Binga Bird, Cold Feet, Sports Briefs, The Colour Keeper* and *the Gwobbles, Weighing it Up* and *Waiting for Annette*. Her work for television includes three episodes of the ABC series *Finders Keepers* .

Sarah Brill*
A number of Sarah's scripts have received workshops or readings at National Young Playwrights Workshops, the WA Young Playwrights Workshop, SWY Theatre Company and the ANPC. Her plays include *Fashion Tips for the Young and Beautiful* and *Fire*, produced at Shopfront Theatre Co-op in Sydney.

Helen Bulley
Over two decades Helen has had eleven radio plays broadcast, *The Empty Stage, The Next Room, Relativity* (Nominated for an AWGIE Award for Best Radio Drama); *Piano Pieces, Autumn Exchanges* (AWGIE Award 1984); *The Man Who Didn't Like Dreaming; Going Home; Song for a Dry Season; Waiting for the Train, Ladies at Lunch* (Winner, ABC Bicentennial Award for Best Original Radio Drama 1988.) Other plays include *Many Happy Returns, A Tale of Our Time* and *The Forest* .

Marion Campbell
Marion has written a number of performance pieces and musical theatre works, including *Ariadne's Understudies* and *Dr Memory in the Dream Home,* both produced in conjunction with the Perth Institute of Contemporary Arts (PICA).

Beatrix Christian*
Beatrix Christian is a Sydney writer who has written for theatre, film and video. Her plays *Spumante Romantica, Inside Dry Water* and *Faust's House* have been produced in NSW, Canberra and Victoria. *Blue Murder* was in Belvoir St.'s 1994 season. She has been an affiliate writer with New Stages at the STC and Co-Artistic Counsel at Belvoir St.

Jennifer Compton*
Jennifer Compton is a poet and playwright who has written over eight works for the stage, including *Crossfire* (formerly *No Man's Land*). On ABC Radio Jennifer has had eleven plays produced including AWGIE winner, *The Goose's Bridle*. As a poet she won the 1995 NSW Writers' Fellowship.

Ruth Conley-Watson
A cabaret/comedy performer and writer, Ruth's works include *Bluebird Express*, a cabaret/comedy piece with music, co-written with Susan Formby.

Janie Conway
Janie's work includes *Add A Grated Laugh or Two, Hitchoni*, a community theatre piece, and *Hotel Australia*, written for the Auto Da Fe company in Sydney.

Jan Cornall*
Jan's writing encompasses a number of different areas: mainstage and fringe theatre, musicals, children's theatre, worksite theatre and film. Her play, *Escape From A Better Place* has had four productions by different companies. She has written the screenplay for Susan Lambert's feature film *Talk*.

Patricia Cornelius
Patricia's produced work includes works for performance, for community groups and TIE; cabaret and music theatre, and pieces for performers and musicians. Her works include: *On the Brink* (Arena Theatre), *Lily and May*, a performance piece, published by Currency Press and performed in many theatres, including Playbox, and *Jack's Daughters* (Theatre Works and at Somebody's Kitchen in Canada). Other produced works include *Electric, The Aftermath, Taxi* (co-written with Vicki Reynolds), *Max, No Fear, Last Drinks, Opa — A Sexual Odyssey, Dusting Our Knees* and *Oh My God I'm Black*.

Cathy Craigie
Cathy has been writing since 1990. Her play *Koori Love* (later *Murri Love*) has been performed at Belvoir Street and by Kooemba Jdarra, Brisbane. *Murri Time*, a children's play, has been performed in Sydney and has toured Queensland. A monologue written by Cathy has been produced by Theatre South and performed at the Festival of Sydney.

Teresa Crea

Teresa is the artistic director of Doppio Teatro and has devised or written the following works: *The Migration of the Madonna, Ricordi, Red like the Devil, Una Fiesta di Nozze* and *Filling the Silence*. She is the inaugural winner of the Federal Government's Cultural Diversity in the Arts Award 1995

Margaret Davis*

Margaret is a writer and director. Her play, *Isis Dreaming* a drama with movement, was seen at The Performance Space and it had a student production at Monash University. Margaret's other plays are *Mad Before Mid-Day, Mary Who? Molly What?* which was commissioned by A Movable Theatre and *Spilling Bodies*, a movement theatre piece.

Alma De Groen

Alma de Groen has been writing since 1970 and has written amongst other works: *The Sweatproof Boy, Going Home, Vocations, The Rivers of China.* and *The Girl who saw Everything.* She has also written for television. Her plays have had major production throughout Australia and are published by Currency Press.

Catherine Fargher*

Catherine's work for theatre includes *I was a Teenage Love Addict*, a group-devised piece which Catherine developed for performance; *Selling Grandma*, an Art and Working Life piece commissioned by Death Defying Theatre; *Salt*, co-written with Helen Duckworth and developed by Playworks and *Future Tense*, a contemporary performance event developed in conjunction with Sidetrack Performance Group.

Margaret Fischer

Margaret Fischer's plays include *Weighing it Up* (co-written with Roxxy Bent, Ollie Black, Anne Brookman); *A Touchy Subject* (co-written with Darrelyn Gunzburg and Ollie Black) published by Tantrum Press, Adelaide 1989; *Home Sweet Home* (co-written with Teresa Crea 1989); *Fabulous Apron Fashion Parade*, *The Gay Divorcee* and *Wanted*. *A Touchy Subject* tours worksites and schools and the other works have all had more than one season in theatres and non-traditional venues.

Josephine Fleming*

Jo Fleming's play, *From the Edge of the Volcano*, received productions at Belvoir St., The Edge Theatre and received Special Mention at the 1989 NSW Premier's Literary Awards. Other works include *Memories, Shadows and Edges* (Fools Gallery, Canberra), *Lunch with Colette* (Interact Theatre Company, Canberra) and *The Wild Colonial Boy Inc.*

Mickey Furuya

Mickey Furuya has created a number of works in collaboration with the performance group The Sydney Front, including their award-winning *First and Last Warning*. She worked with Clare Grant and others on Clare's *Woman in the Wall*.

Jodi Gallagher

Much of Jodi's work has been developed by her working with actors, sometimes during rehearsals she directed herself. Her works include: *I Broke his Coffee Cup*, a one-woman show performed in Melbourne and Adelaide, *Glorious Technicolour* and *The Method*, which received productions at La Mama and Playbox. Other works include *Queenie, The Pale, Banshee, Not Quite Anaïs* and *Web* .

Christine Gillespie

Christine Gillespie has written short stories, articles and non-fiction in addition to works for theatre and film. She is currently developing a play script, *White Stars*, and developed and presented the English commentary for a play *Mulgi Zali Ho* (*A Girl is Born*) performed in the Marathi language by an Indian feminist drama group in Adelaide, Sydney and Melbourne in 1994.

Venetia Gillot

Salt Fire Water, a cross-cultural work, was group developed from a project initiated by Venetia. It has had performances at Brown's Mart Theatre, Darwin and The Space, at the Adelaide Festival Centre.

Marlish Glorie

Marlish has written and performed her own cabaret work and has also written three plays, two of which, *Changes in Attitude* and *Zoo Life*, were commissioned by a TIE company. Other works include *Onder De Appleboom* (Dutch — *Beneath the Appletree*), *Midnight Matchmakers* and *The Garden Party* .

Sharon Guest

Sharon Guest has written two plays, workshopped at a number of venues in Sydney.

Suzanne Hawley

Suzanne's writing credits include scripts for theatre, TV and film. Plays produced include *Concrete Palaces, Mummy Loves You, Betty Ann Jewel* and *Hitler Had a Mummy Too*. Her work has been published by Currency Press.

Leila Hayes

Leila has written about a dozen plays, drama, comedy, for youth and community theatre.

Claire Haywood

Claire is a writer and director. Her play, *Table for One*, has received productions by Hunter Valley Theatre Company, Ensemble Theatre, Jigsaw Theatre Company and toured to Victoria and Western Australia. *Christmas Day* was staged by the Q Theatre and Hunter Valley Theatre Company. Other works include *Dangerous Curve* and *It Couldn't Happen to Me* .

Debra Hely

Deborah has workshopped *Indoor Weather, Georgie* and *After the Sunsets.*

Dorothy Hewett

Playwright, novelist, poet and screen writer, Dorothy Hewett is the recipient of numerous awards and honours. Her plays include: *This Old Man Comes Rolling Home* (1965); *Mrs Porter and the Angel* (1970); *The Chapel Perilous* (1971); *Bon-Bons and Roses for Dolly* (1972); *Catspaw* (1974); *The Tatty Hollow Story* (1976); *Joan* (1975); *The Golden Oldies* (1976); *Pandora's Cross* (1975); *The Man from Mukinupin* (1979); *The Fields of Heaven* (1981); *Golden Valley* (1982); *Song of the Seals* (1983); *Christina's World* (1982); *The Rising of Pete Marsh* (1988); *Zoo* (1991). *The Jarrabin Trilogy* is a work-in-progress commissioned by State Theatre Company of WA.

Pauline Hosking

Pauline has had two plays at La Mama, one at Melbourne Writers Theatre, and one performed by several amateur groups. *The Gallery Gamble* and *Snakes and Ladders* have been published by Bushfire Press, and the latter is studied by Year 12 Theatre Studies and Drama Students, VCE, Victoria, 1995. Five of her children's plays have been published by the NSW Education Department.

Mary Hutchison

Mary has written for a range of companies, including puppet companies and youth theatres and a number of radio plays. Her works include: *Child of the Hurricane, Did you Say Love?, Bogong, Salt Mustard Vinegar Pepper, Break and Enter* and the radio play *Three Pieces.* Mary is working on *Mum's the Word* for Company Skylark.

Sue Ingleton*

Sue Ingleton is an accomplished performer who has a number of published and performed works to her credit including: *From Here to Maternity, Mothers Courage, Blood and Milk Show, Characters 2, Strip Jack Naked* and *Near Ms's* plus a large body of standup comedy material. Her work *The Passion...and its deep connection with Lemon Delicious Pudding*, developed with Playworks, was produced by Playbox in 1995 and published by Currency Press.

Noëlle Janaczewska*

Noëlle writes for theatre, radio and print. Recent plays and radio scripts include: *Yungaburra Rd, The Marie Curie Chat Show, Blood Orange* and *The History of Water/Huyen Thoai Mot Giong Nuoc,* staged in London and Ottawa and published by Currency Press.

Julie Janson*

Julie began writing and directing plays in remote Aboriginal communities in the Northern Territory in the 1970's. *Gunjies,* a play about black deaths in custody, was produced at Belvoir St. in 1993. Other works are *Black Mary* and *Lotus War,* presented at the 1995 Sydney Asian Festival, Belvoir Street. Julie is writing a new play, *Tears of the Poppy.*

Patricia Johnson

Patricia Johnson's writing credits include works for the stage and for television. Her plays include *Gladbags,* which was staged by Ensemble Productions, the Hole in the Wall in Perth and the Q Theatre as well as touring in NSW and Qld; *The Cocky on the Lawn, And the Bestman Makes Three* and *You Must Remember This.*

Patricia Jones

Patricia's work has received development assistance from Griffin Theatre.

Barbara Karpinski*

Barbara is a writer and multi-media artist and has performed her own satiric and erotic characterisations at venues around Sydney. She wrote and directed the film *Liquid Guns and Ammo* and her work *Fufu Fairy Dreaming* received assistance from Playworks and was presented at the *In the Pink* Series at Belvoir St.

Jenny Kemp

Jenny Kemp's plays, all of which she has directed herself, are: *The Point Isn't To Tell You, Sheila Alone, The White Hotel,* a stage adaptation of D.M. Thomas' novel and *Goodnight Sweet Dreams. Call of the Wild* was performed for the Spoleto Festival at Church Theatre in 1989 and toured to Belvoir St. *Remember* was produced at the Gasworks in 1993. Jenny's new work *The Black-Sequinned Dress* has been commissioned by Barrie Kosky for the 1996 Adelaide Festival.

Stella Kent*

Her plays *Because* and*Demons* have been broadcast by ABC Radio. Another radio play, *Tales of One City* received the 1995 AWGIE for radio drama.

Margaret Kirby*

My Body. My Blood, produced at St Paul's Cathedral Chapter House, Melbourne, has been published by Currency Press. Margaret's other plays are: *Bachelor Rock* , *The Predator*, a thirty minute narrative, and *Threads*, a

narrative drama on an epic scale which Margaret is currently developing, as well as a new play, *Aliens*.

Anna Lall

Her play *Situation Critical* had a reading at Melbourne Writers Theatre. *No More Tigers*, a one-act comedy was produced at Noosa Arts Festival, 1984. Her latest work, *Bring on the Lions* , is a drama for radio and live performance.

Tobsha Learner*

Tobsha Learner writes for theatre, film, radio and television. Her plays, produced by theatre companies throughout Australia, include: *Witchplay, S.N.A.G., Miracle, Tendril,Wolf, Angels, Mistress* Her recent work includes *The Glass Mermaid*, presented by Playbox in 1994 from a QTC commission and *Seven Acts of Love as witnessed by a Cat* directed by Tobsha for Budinski's Theate of Exile. Her radio plays include *Volkov* and *Lionheart* (silver medal at the 1993 New York International Radio Competition). She is published by Currency Press.

Carolyn Logan

Carolyn's play *Breast Stroke* was performed by SWY Theatre and her works *Baby Baby* and *Off the Wall* have been broadcast by ABC's Radio National.

Maryanne Lynch

Maryanne has written a number of performance pieces: *Ghostings* (Metro Arts Theatre and La Boite Theatre), *The Waiting Room* (Metro Arts Theatre) and *Starting Point* (La Boite Theatre). Her radio play *The Lives of Ada* was broadcast by Radio National.

Alison Lyssa*

In addition to works for the theatre, Alison writes fiction and poetry. Her plays include *The Year of the Migrant, Pinball, The Boiling Frog ,The Hospital Half Hour and Who'd've Thought?* Her work has been published by Currency Press and Methuen. Her new play *Where There's A Will* will be showcased by Playworks in 1995

Tes Lyssiotis

Tes Lyssiotis is a director and writer. Her works, many of which are bi-lingual or multi-lingual include: *But I Like it Here, Girls Talk, Come to Australia They Said, Hotel Bonegilla, On The Line, The Journey, A White Sports Coat, and The Forty Lounge Cafe* (which has also been adapted for radio).

Mardi McConnochie*

Mardi's plays have appeared in seasons of new writing with Unley Youth Theatre (*Bareback Riders*) and Vitalstatistix (*The Towers*). Her commissioned work for Unley, *Toxic Girls*, was presented at The Space, Adelaide and in Sydny for the Gay & Lesbian Mardi Gras Festival. *Vestal Beach* was staged by Tryst Productions.

Karin Mainwaring

Karin's first play, *Binge*, was staged by Griffin Theatre. *The Rain Dancers* received productions by the Sydney Theatre Company, La Boite and has also been produced in New Zealand. *Stiffs* was produced by the State Theatre Company of South Australia and will be by Sydney Theatre Company in 1996.

Vicki Moore

Vicki's performance piece, *An Evening with Catherine Helen Spence* has been performed at Belvoir St. Theatre Downstairs.

Peta Murray

Peta Murray's play *Wallflowering* has received many productions in Australia and has also been performed in New Zealand and the UK. Peta has been commissioned by a number of theatre companies; productions include *Spitting Chips, This Dying Business, Rubbish, The Flying Flopps, The Diver, One Woman's Song, The Source* and *The Keys to the Animal Room* (Gold AWGIE 1994). Her work is published by Currency Press.

Joanna Murray-Smith

Plays include *Atlanta, Ridge's Lovers, Love-Child, Honour, Takers* and *Angry Young Penguins*. Joanna's work has been produced by many companies, including Playbox, La Mama and Griffin. Her work has been published by Currency Press.

Heather Nimmo

Heather writes for theatre, film and television. Among the 18 of her plays that have been performed throughout Australia are *Hope, Mean Deeds, Boots, One Small Step* and the musicals *A Touch of Midas* and *Beijing Spring*. Her plays for children include *Junk, Mebabel's Story, Fossils* and the puppet play, *Gammer*.

Fiona Navilly

Fiona is co-director of Canberra's Tango 160 whose works for theatre include a number of plays for young people: *Baked Potatoes, SPLASH!, Just One Drop* and *Spanner in the Works. Solitude My Mother. A Glimpse of Olegas Truchanas* is a solo theatre piece.

Anna North*

Anna North's play *Fear of Angels* has been workshopped and showcased by Playworks.

Debra Oswald

Debra Oswald is a scriptwriter in television, film, radio and theatre. Her playwrighting credits include *Lumps, Gary's House, Going Under, Dags* and *Two-Way Mirror*. Her work has been seen at the Q Theatre, Griffin Theatre, Nimrod Theatre, Troupe Theatre and Canberra Youth Theatre. *Dags* has been published by Currency Press and in the USA and UK.

Dina Panozzo*

Dina is a performer and writer. Her work *Varda Che Bruta...Poretta (Look How Ugly She Is...Poor Thing)*, a tri-lingual solo performance piece for live and video self, was produced by the writer in collaboration with Open City and received productions in Sydney, Melbourne and Adelaide.

Deborah Pollard

Deborah's solo works include *Eat Cake* and *Mother Tongue Interference*. She has created a number of works in collaboration with Victoria Spence, most notably*The Fall of the Roman Empire* and *Dripping With Ennui*. Deborah has recently created collaborative performance works in Indonesia.

Sue-Ann Post

Australia's only six foot, gap-toothed, lesbian stand up comic. Her one woman show *A Bit of a Postscript* has successfully toured to Sydney, Adelaide, Canberra and New Zealand and another show, *Grumpy Old Dyke*, has been performed in Melbourne.

Therese Radic

Therese Radic is a playwright, biographer and musicologist, whose works have received many productions in Australia and overseas. Plays include *Some of My Best Friends Are Women, A Whip Round for Percy Grainger, Madame Mao, Peach Melba and The Emperor Regrets*. Her plays have been published by Currency Press.

Monica Raszewski*

Forest, a play for radio, has received a number of readings and workshops and will be included in the 1995 Playwright's Conference. She is currently researching a new play and working on a novel.

Hannie Rayson

Hannie is the author of *Please Return to Sender, Leave it Til Monday, Mary, Room to Move* and a teleplay, *Sloth*, which is part of the ABC series, *The Seven Deadly Sins*. Her play, *Hotel Sorrento* was commissioned by Playbox and was also presented by the Sydney Theatre Company. It has won a number of awards and has also been made into a feature film. *Falling From Grace* was jointly commissioned by Playbox Theatre and QTC and the production has had a national tour, and is published by Currency.

Sally Richardson

Sally's works for theatre include *Picasso and Francoise, Five Fingers, So Is It a Lover?, I Am Nijinsky* (which incorporates dance and film), and the solo performance piece *Kamarade. Of He and She* is a piece for radio. Sally is a former director of Playworks and currently Script Development Officer at Stages in WA.

Virginia Jane Rose

Virginia's plays include *If the Shoes Fit, Loaded Dice, Freedom of the Heart*, produced by Terrapin Puppet Theatre and *Malache: Despatches from another World*, a one woman play commissioned by La Troupe Theatre, Sydney. The play has had several productions throughout Australia and also a season in repertory at the Contemporary Theatre of Syracuse, New York.

Annette Rups-Eyland

Annette is a choreographer, performer and writer whose performance pieces include *For Eve, Song In a Strange Land* and *Dark Fire.*

Sonia Ryan*

Sonia's work *The Seer and the Seen* was showcased by Playworks in 1994. Other works include *The Hill, Clot* and *The Last Judgement: A Passion Play About the Olympic Bid with God In It*. In 1995, *Pirates!* and *Upon Pain of Your Displeasure* have been performed at the Australian National Maritime Museum, Sydney.

Jill Shearer
Although she has also written poetry and short stories, Jill is best known as the author of some18 plays including *The Expatriate, The Kite, Stephen, Nocturne, The Boat* and *The Family*. *Shimada*, following productions by the Melbourne Theatre Company and Queensland Theatre Company, had a season on Broadway. Jill's work has been published by Currency Press and Play Lab Press.

Sandra Shotlander
Sandra is a short-story writer, playwright and actor. Her productions include *Framework, Blind Salome* (which she directed in Melbourne in 1985), and *Is That You Nancy?* which was produced at Belvoir St. Theatre and broadcast on ABC-FM.

Elizabeth Spencer
Her play *Where My Mind Doesn't Follow Me*, developed by Perth Writers Laboratory and Stages, was produced at the Actors Centre 1995.

Suzanne Spunner
Suzanne is a playwright, designer and dramaturg. She was a founding member of Home Cooking Company and her works include *Not Still Lives, Running Up a Dress, Safe 'n' Sound, Dragged Screaming to Paradise, Overcome by Chlorine* and *The Accompanist*. *The Ingkata's Wife* (1990), which she wrote and designed, brings together performance, epic drama and music theatre. Suzanne also writes for film.

Jennie Swain*
Jennie's play, *There Goes the Neighbourhood*, a music theatre work, was produced at La Mama and has also been adapted for radio. *Pills I Love 'em to Death* has been staged in Melbourne and Sydney. Plays written for community groups include *Rituals, Rhythms and Routines* and *Never Trust a Lyrebird*.

Peta Tait*
Peta Tait is the author of *Converging Realities: Feminism in Australian Theatre*. Plays include *Deadlock* which was part of New Australian Works at Griffin Theatre in 1988 and produced at James Cook University.She co-wrote *Mesmerised* with Matra Robertson and *Appearing in Pieces* with The Partyline produced at The Performance Space.

Katherine Thomson*
Katherine Thomson is an actor and writer. Her plays, which have received numerous productions throughout Australia, include *Tonight We Anchor in Twofold Bay, Barmaids* (AWGIE Award 1992), *A Sporting Chance, Darlinghurst Nights* and *Diving for Pearls* (Victorian Premier's Literary Award for Drama, 1991). Her work is published by Currency Press. She also writes for television.

Alana Valentine*
Alana is a writer and director. Her play, *Southern Belle* won the 1994 ANPC/New Drmatists Award, which enabled her to workshop the script with New Dramatists in New York. Other plays include *Multiple Choice, Shudder* and *Swellings*. A number of Alana's works for radio have been broadcast by the ABC.

Jenny Weight*
Jenny's play *The Revivalists* was showcased by Playworks and has been produced by Vitalstatistix in Adelaide. She also writes performance poetry and prose.

Linden Wilkinson*
Linden Wilkinson is a performer and writer. Plays include *Back On, Family Favourites, Sleeping Partners,* and *Nice Girls* which received productions in Sydney and Melbourne. Linden also writes for television.

Paula Williams
Paula's works for the stage include *Sha, Spirit of the Cave, Close Encounters On a Beach, Patterns* and *Silver Sails*.

Sue Woolf
Sue Woolf adapts her fiction for the stage. Her first novel *Painted Woman* (Allen & Unwin) has been produced at Belvoir Street (1991) and La Boite (1994) and heard on Radio National (1995). Her second novel *Leaning Towards Infinity* (Random House, 1995) has been read at the New York Women's Project and at the University of Iowa

Catherine Zimdahl*
Catherine writes for theatre, film and television. For theatre her works include *Family Running for Mr. Whippy*, which has been staged by the Sydney Theatre Company and Playbox. Film work includes *Sparks* (which has won a number of awards) and *Life On Earth As I Know It*.

Others involved in this publication:

Colleen Chesterman
Colleen is a writer and editor. When Deputy Director of the NSW Women's Coordination Unit, she was one of the initiators of the 1982 Women and Arts Festival and was on the Reseach Committee. She has worked as a consultant for the Australia Council, has been on the Company B Board and is currently on Playworks Board. She is writing a book on growing up female in Sydney after World War II.

Tanya Gerstle
Tanya is a performer, director and teacher. She has co-created more than 15 group and solo preformance pieces either directing or performing them in Britain, Europe and Australia. Her most recent performance work includes playing Paulina, in *Death and the Maiden*, by Ariel Dorfmann.

Verity Laughton
Verity is a South Australian playwright, dramaturg and short story writer. Her plays include *Solo* and *Crimson Roses*. Her first collection of short stories, *Knife On Silk*, will be published in 1996.

The following writers' biographies are detailed in Playworks' Directory:
Donna Abela, Jane Ahlquist, Marilyn Allen, Lissa Benyon, Susie Boisjoux, Elizabeth Eldridge, Kathleen Mary Fallon, Anni Finsterer, Merryn Johns, Linda Neil, Jennifer Paynter, Alison Rooney and Alice Spigelman.

Writers receiving Playworks assistance 1994/95:
Belinda Bradley, Sarah Brill, Anni Finsterer, Sara Hardy, Noelle Janaczewska, Melina Marchetti, Christine Phillips, Matra Robertson, Alana Valentine.

Writers offered Playworks assistance 1995/96
Annie Bilton, Merlinda Bobis, Susie Bromfield, Bronwyn Calcutt, Nuala Cassidy, Angela Costi, Kathryn Denney, Rachel Guy, Corrie Hosking, Sally Irwin, Alison Lyssa, Clare Mendes, Eliane Morel, Fawnia Mountford, Virginia Jane Rose, Sonia Ryan and Annette Tesoriero.

Playworks Committee members 1985-1995
Virginia Baxter, Lissa Benyon, Beverley Blankenship, Colleen Chesterman, Eliza Chidiac, Beatrix Christian, Jennifer Compton, Jessica Douglas-Henry, Jo Fleming, Anne Hinchcliffe, Ros Horin, Lilian Horler, Clare Grant, Noelle Janaczewska, Brigid Kitchin, Jacqui Lo, Alison Lyssa, Anna Messariti, Pamela Payne, Deborah Pollard, Marion Potts, Sally Richardson, Jane Schwager, Francesca Smith, Alison Summers, Helen Swan, Pam Thompson, Katherine Thomson, Christina Totos, Jane Ulman, Alana Valentine, Anna Volska, Linden Wilkinson, Margaret Williams, Carol Woodrow.